Praise for "People Power"

66 An exciting, uplifting, empowering book. These principles really do work, whether you're trying to get ahead in a job, establish a business, or raise $100 million. **99**

> **Scott DeGarmo**
> Editor-in-Chief and Publisher
> *Success*

66 Warm, personal, and inspiring! Its message of service can help you create quality connections that will last a lifetime. **99**

> **Beth Everts**
> President
> Park National Bank–Westchase

66 Provides valuable and practical information on how to develop strong networks. These principles serve a vital role in the professional development of our young managers. **99**

> **J. Terry Strange**
> Managing Partner
> KPMG Peat Marwick–Southwest

66 This idea-packed book shows you how to network better and easier than ever before. Get it, read it, and start applying its powerful principles in your life today! **99**

> **Brian Tracy**
> Author of *Selling Strategies*

66 *An excellent resource for anyone who wants to build a strong network that keeps on working.* **99**

John Gray
Author of *Men Are from Mars, Women Are from Venus*

66 *Easy to read, understand, and put into practice. Its content would be beneficial to the experienced business-person as well as those just beginning their careers.* **99**

Lorry F. Harju
President and CEO
American Institute of Banking, Houston

66 *Every penny you earn in your entire lifetime is made possible by the cooperation of other people. People Power offers life-affirming insights to help you become richer in every way.* **99**

Michael LeBoeuf
Author of *How to Win Customers and Keep Them for Life*

66 *A refreshing acknowledgment of the power of people in this age of technology. Donna's book shows us how to nurture our relationships to naturally enhance our personal and business lives.* **99**

Beth Wolff
President
Beth Wolff & Associates Realtors

66 *Great 'how-to' book about the really important funda-mentals of career and personal networking. A must-read for people who want to experience 'authentic' success.* **99**

Ivan Misner, Ph.D.
Author of *The World's Best-Known Marketing Secret: Building Your Business with Word-of-Mouth Marketing*

Donna Fisher

PEOPLE POWER

12 POWER PRINCIPLES TO ENRICH YOUR BUSINESS, CAREER & PERSONAL NETWORKS

DONNA FISHER

Coauthor of
***Power Networking:
55 Secrets for
Personal & Professional Success***

AUSTIN, TEXAS

People Power
12 Power Principles to Enrich
Your Business, Career & Personal Networks

Bard Press
1515 Capital of Texas Hwy, Ste. 107
Austin, TX 78746
Phone: (512) 329-8373   Fax: (512) 329-6051

Ordering Information
To order additional copies, contact your local bookstore or call (800) 934-9675. Quantity discounts are available.

ISBN 1-885167-11-3   trade paperback

Library of Congress Cataloging-in-Publication Data

Fisher, Donna.
    People power : 12 power principles to enrich your business, career & personal networks / Donna Fisher.
        p.   cm.
    Includes bibliographical references and index.
    1. Success in business.   2. Career development.   3. Social networks.   4. Interpersonal relations.   5. Interprofessional relations.   I. Title.
    HF5386.F4155 1995
    650.1—dc20   95-31726
                                                                         CIP

The author may be contacted at the following address:
    6524 San Felipe, PMB #138, Houston, TX 77057-2611
    Toll free: (800) 934-9675 Direct: (713) 267-3914
    e-mail: donna@donnafisher.com
    www.donnafisher.com

Credits

Copyediting: Helen Hyams
Proofreading: Helen Hyams, Deborah Costenbader, Leslie Coplin
Text design: Suzanne Pustejovsky
Cover design: Suzanne Pustejovsky
Composition/production: Round Rock Graphics
Index: Linda Webster

First printing: October 1995
Second printing: April 1997
Third printing: March 1998
Fourth printing: June 1999
Fifth printing: October 2000

CONTENTS

Part III: Strengthening Your Networking Power

Part IV: Polishing Your Networking Skills

9

THANKS TO MY NETWORK

AS I GO THROUGH LIFE and face my own challenges and opportunities, I gain a greater appreciation for my friends, family, and business associates—my network. That appreciation becomes as evident during times when I need moral support or personal advice as it is when I need new business or professional support. I have learned about the value of having a support system of personal and professional friends as I progress along my career path and through life. I will share with you throughout this book some of my stories and the stories of many other people just like you and me. These stories show the impact networking can have on your life on a daily basis. Thanks to all the people who shared their stories and experiences with me: Lilly Aranda, Regina Bruce, David Burrows, Becky Easley, Debbie Golden, Alan and Cindy Goldsberry, Elaine Gray, John Hall, Steve Hammett, David Lallier, Joleen McMaster, Peggy McQuaid, Marianne Smith, Judy Vitucci, Cheryl Watson, Pippa Wiley, and Sally Wilson.

I also want to thank Katherine Ashby, Mary Ann Bryan, Kathy Butera, Andrew Connell, Cathy Daly, Dana Morrison, Sandy Musson, Doug Smith, Stan Tyler, Tess Yevka, Byron Zaner, and the members of The Windsor Club for their friendship, continual support, and encouragement.

Thanks to the many others who graciously shared their time in reviewing various versions of the manuscript: Barbie Adams, Amy Backlas, Randy Blanchard, Bill Browning, Carol Ann Dovi, Beth Everts, Thomas Farmer, Naomi Karten, Chris L. Means, Mary Lynn Moore, Phil Morabito, Alice Ostrower, Randon Reaves, Meredith Saidel, Guy Simpler, Woodrow W. Vaughan III, and Joe Vitale.

Special thanks to my mom, Betty Fisher, for being one of my best friends and biggest supporters.

I am especially grateful to Ray Bard, Scott Bard, and Leslie Stephen for the loving dedication with which you birth a book—it is a pleasure to work with you. Thanks also to Helen Hyams for doing a wonderful job of cleaning up my writing and to Suzanne Pustejovsky for your beautiful design work.

I continue to learn about building a strong support system, for I am building a network for life. The power of networking lies in the people you bring into your life. I have learned that networking addresses our basic need as humans to belong, to feel part of a community, to have a sense of connection. I have discovered that networking is vital in our lives! I appreciate the opportunity to share through this book my discoveries, thoughts, and experiences with you.

The power of networking
is in the human interaction
and the personal value generated
by the interaction.

—Donna Fisher

REALIZING THE RICHNESS
OF YOUR NETWORKS

*❝**A**lone we can do so little,*
together we can do so much. ❞

—Helen Keller

STOP AND THINK FOR A MOMENT. What do the following things have in common?

Your first job

The last movie you saw

Your most important business deal

Your car

Your accountant

Your spouse or lover

The last book you read

The biggest decision you ever made about your health

Your auto mechanic

Your special vacation spot

Your attorney

Your computer

Your favorite restaurant

Your present job

Your physician

The answer is people. Most of us make both important and everyday life choices because of other people. It is almost always another person who tells us about a great job opening, raves about a favorite getaway spot, or introduces us to a special person. When you need an attorney, a physician, or an accountant, a good mechanic, or some advice about which computer to buy, you call on someone you know. The essential ingredient in networking is people. The power of people joining together because of a common purpose, a mutual goal, or a similar passion is instrumental in the growth and development of healthy, productive families, communities, businesses, organizations, and countries.

YOUR LIFETIME NETWORK

No matter what your career path or role in life, your ability to build a strong support system will be a key factor in your success. If you're in sales, the ability to build strong client relationships is instrumental in developing repeat business, new business, and referral business. If you're among the growing number of people starting their own businesses, your network will provide your most effective marketing tool. If you work in the corporate world, you need to create your own job security by building a support system of contacts. And if you are looking for a job, your personal and professional contacts will help you to find that ideal job in a timely and efficient manner.

Networking is a lifelong process of meeting people, making contacts, developing friendships, and building professional relationships. Your network is unlimited. It includes people you grew up with, people you went to school with, family, friends, clients, neighbors, and co-workers. Networking has been around forever and always will be. But networking is very often misunderstood and misused. If you've been skeptical of networking, I ask you to take a fresh look. Take this opportunity to enhance your people power by developing a networking style that is consistent, gracious, and powerful.

This book outlines twelve power principles for a style of networking that exemplifies a natural desire to belong, to be

15

part of a community, to have a support system, and to relate to others in a harmonious and mutually supportive manner. Once you have mastered these principles and know how to apply them in every aspect of your life, you will have a rich, powerful support system that you can call on anytime, for anything. The information, exercises, and stories in this book can assist you in starting, building, or enriching your network. It is up to you to take these ideas and implement them successfully.

THE PATH BEFORE YOU

Everyone already networks to some degree. However, many people are networking "dabblers." They network haphazardly, a little bit here and there. Sometimes it seems to work and sometimes it doesn't, but they don't really know how to improve their results. Maybe they don't realize that the way they ask for help turns people off. Or they expect immediate results and miss out on the long-range opportunities that are produced through persistence and consistency. Networking involves learning how and when to approach people, how and when to offer support, how and when to ask for help.

Many people who are truly masterful at networking do so in a very quiet, yet powerful, manner. Their interpersonal skills are so well tuned, their style is so natural, their approach is so graceful that you may have difficulty defining exactly why they are so effective at continually bringing in new business, making new friends, or finding new opportunities. The skills we use to interact, communicate, and relate to people are vital to our ability to function in the world, to have positive self-esteem, to adjust to changes and challenges in our lives.

Haphazard networking produces sporadic, short-lived results. Purposeful, consistent networking generates a support system that keeps on giving for a lifetime. You have the ability to develop a style of networking that produces consistent, long-lasting, and life-enhancing results. This book shows you how.

PART

I

NETWORKING

FOR LIFE

CHAPTER TWO

THE TRUE POWER
OF NETWORKING

*" It is one of the most beautiful compensations
of this life that no one can sincerely try to
help another without helping himself. "*

—Ralph Waldo Emerson

NETWORKING IS AS SIMPLE AS FRIEND-
SHIP and as complex as matchmak-
ing. It is gathering, collecting, and
distributing information, being a
resource for others, and learning
how to call on the resources in
your network. Networking is choosing interdependence over isolation
and realizing the power of cooperation over competition. It links people and information to one another
for the mutual benefit of everyone
involved. Networking provides a
form of community, family, and
camaraderie.

Although networking is obviously valuable in building a business
or finding a job, its importance goes much deeper. It satisfies
a basic need to be connected, to belong, and to contribute. It
is not just a good idea for business. It is a life-affirming process and a vital ingredient for success and happiness. We exist
as part of a vast and intricate web of connections. They bring

us joy and peace, motivation and rich ideas. They enrich all aspects of our lives.

THE LINK BETWEEN NETWORKING AND HEALTH

Networking is not just a good practice for lifetime success and satisfaction; it is a vital ingredient for health. It provides a basis for mental, physical, spiritual, and emotional well-being. A strong support system contributes to a sense of connectedness, security, confidence, and peace of mind. According to epidemiologist Lisa Berkman of Yale University, people who have strong emotional and social ties live longer than people who score low on her "social network index." James S. House, a University of Michigan sociologist, draws a similar conclusion after his study of two thousand adults. His report verifies that there is "a death rate twice as high in unsociable women as sociable women, and up to three times as high in unsociable men as compared to sociable men." Our ability to relate, connect, and interact with others is a primary aspect of who we are as social beings.

"There isn't any one relationship that's critical," Berkman believes. "What is critical is having—or not having—close connections with people." The types of relationships we have are of the utmost importance. Relationships based on an attitude of altruism have a positive impact on our health and longevity. The Institute for the Advancement of Health also reports a scientific relationship between helping and health. When you help someone else, the positive effect is a sense of satisfaction for having contributed and been of value. In a study of three thousand volunteers, Allan Luks, former executive director of the Institute for the Advancement of Health and director of Big Brothers/Big Sisters in New York, found: "People who help others frequently report better health than people who don't." A caring attitude is a common denominator for experiencing a happy, productive, and satisfying life.

21

THE LINK BETWEEN NETWORKING AND CAREER SECURITY

Job security is a thing of the past. You can, however, develop your own career security by building and maintaining a support system of professional contacts. When I went to work for Exxon Company USA after graduating from college, my family's response was very positive because they thought I would have job security. You may have thought the same thing at some time in your career. But things have changed in the job market. Companies no longer can say that they will take care of people indefinitely. Your job security comes from your employability, visibility, and marketability. You must stay in charge of your career by continually developing your skills, your network, and your employability.

A strong support system helps you to cope with the stress of dealing day-to-day with the uncertainty and chaos that is present in so many companies and industries. When you have a strong network, you are less likely to feel anxious and threatened by the possibility of change. You are therefore able to function in a more productive, positive, and supportive manner even during difficult times. When you do not have a strong network, you are more likely to feel scared and threatened; you may tend to withdraw, isolate yourself, become territorial, and function less effectively as a team player. Take charge of your career—build your network whether or not you plan to change jobs or careers. Create a safety net for the unexpected while at the same time laying a foundation for the career growth that will meet your aspirations.

THE LINK BETWEEN NETWORKING AND SALES

Networking adds a personal touch to the numbers game of sales. It provides a proven, systematic approach to making contacts with people through a common interest, friend, or associate. Sales result when people connect with people. Any business that wants to survive and thrive must keep its attention on marketing, sales, and business development.

Marketing is the means by which you create visibility for yourself, your business, your products, and your services. Word-of mouth marketing happens when people tell others about your products and services. Networking will get your word out to people efficiently, generate results quickly, and continuously build momentum. You can have the greatest product or service in the world, but if people don't know about it, what good does it do? Every satisfied customer can give you more positive exposure.

Networking softens and enhances the sales process by providing a way to make "warm calls" and even "hot calls," rather than cold calls. A warm call is a call to someone you know through one of your contacts. Even though you may not know the person yourself, it is a warm call because someone has recommended you. Your mutual relationship establishes a common ground and that first stepping-stone of credibility.

A hot call is a call made with a strong and definite recommendation and an obvious fit. For example, I recently made a hot call after I was contacted by Jolene McMaster, president of Market Profiles of Houston. She said that she had given my name to Peggy McQuaid at the law firm of Arnold, White & Durkee because they were looking for someone to lead an educational and motivational program for their paralegals. This was a hot lead because a specific need was expressed and I had been recommended by someone in the legal community. I called right away, found out more about the firm's interests, sent them a packet of information, and was booked for the engagement within a week. How great to have results happen so easily and quickly!

If you can develop the skill and discipline to be successful through cold-calling, you can multiply your results through networking. You never know when or where your next prospect or client might appear; the more warm calls you make, the greater the chance of developing hot calls that produce easy, quick opportunities.

Even though networking is a powerful process that leads to sales, you cannot expect every contact or person in

23

your network to become a client or customer. Even sales expert Jeffrey Gitomer says, "Every networking contact need not lead to a sale. New information, hot connections, trends and support are just as important in network building as sales. People will do business with you once they get to know you and see you perform. Mature relationships breed sales."

One of the reasons networking has gotten a bad reputation is because many people are selling in the name of networking. People buy based on a level of trust, rapport, and relationship. Done correctly, networking can result in a higher closing rate, more referral business, and long-term clients. Even if you are not a sales professional, networking is a great way to develop your ability to be a resource for new business and continued business development. The process of meeting people and creating visibility for yourself lays the groundwork for people to learn about your products and services. Develop a strong and broad base of contacts and let your network do the selling.

■ REAPING THE BENEFITS

You may be interested in networking to generate sales, business, and more money. You may want to use it to find a job, start a new business, expand into a new region or market. You could be interested in networking to find a mate, hire new employees, or locate a mentor. There are many reasons to build a support system and thus many ways to benefit. The benefits you reap will directly correlate with how effectively you learn to develop an easy, natural networking style in all areas of your life.

Ways Your Network Can Be of Value and Benefit:

- ☑ It is a source of inspiration.
- ☑ It is a self-esteem and confidence booster.
- ☑ It promotes ease in meeting and talking to people.
- ☑ It helps you to stay on track with your goals.

- ☑ It gives you access to information and contacts that would not otherwise be available.
- ☑ It provides strong friendships and moral support.
- ☑ It gives you a sense of security and connectedness.
- ☑ It gives you a greater awareness of the value of friends and contacts.
- ☑ It gives you a way to contribute to the success of others.
- ☑ It provides easier access to people and information.

 Recognize Your Support System

Answer the following questions to recognize the power of your support system:

25

How does my support system contribute to my health and well-being?

How does my support system contribute to my career advancement?

How does my support system contribute to my sales or the growth of my business?

In what other ways would I like networking to enhance my life?

THE TRUE SPIRIT OF NETWORKING

Networking Is Not:

Selling

Impersonal

Passing out business cards

Using other people

For people who "need" help

A technique

Another "thing to do"

An obligation

Keeping score

Being abrasive and brash

Name-dropping

Glorifying yourself

Gaining power over people

Manipulation or intimidation

Restrictive of gender, race, or age

Impressing others

Time-consuming

Aggressiveness

Only for the outgoing

Using people

Networking Is:

Making contacts

Getting to know people and developing relationships

Exchanging business cards when there is a reason to stay in touch

Utilizing resources for mutual benefit

For people who are motivated to accomplish their goals and dreams

An attitude of support and camaraderie

A blend of attitude, habits, and skills; a way of life

A natural human tendency to want to give and contribute

Giving with no obligations or expectations

Being gracious

Sharing information and contacts with integrity

Expressing yourself

Giving power to people

Asking and offering in a nondemanding manner

Inclusive of everyone

Promoting something of value

A time-saver

Persistence and patience

Appropriate for all personality styles

Serving people

Networking is the way you interact and relate to the people, the world, and the opportunities around you.

CONNECTING THROUGH LIFE'S UPS AND DOWNS

❝ The love of a friend can be what we need to get through a hard time, just as a friend can make a good time even better. ❞

—Muriel James

T

HE TIME TO CALL ON YOUR NET-
WORK is all the time—in tough times,
good times, times of success, times
of difficulty. Life is like a roller coast-
er. Sometimes we are at the bottom
and it looks like an impossible climb
up. At other times we are at the top
and feeling great! It is important to
network throughout the cycle. When
you're at the bottom, you may be
calling on your network a lot. When
you're on the top of the curve, you
may be giving to your network a
great deal. During difficult times, it's
often easy to think, "Well, how can I call on them *now?*" Yet
"now" is always the right time. Over the big picture things
will even out. Just as the ocean naturally ebbs and flows, there
is an ebb and flow in giving and receiving support. Build a
support system that is strong and solid so that when you need
help or support, your network will be there.

YOU NEVER KNOW . . .

I have met with two women friends on a regular basis for over four years. Our monthly potluck is a time to talk, share, cry, and laugh about anything and everything that's going on in our lives. We enjoy each other's company and the opportunity to talk openly and intimately. I have learned over the years to let my friends know when I need help. So at one of our monthly gatherings, I told them that I had been procrastinating about going in to get my baseline mammogram, even though I was several years beyond the recommended age. Several months later Cathy called and asked, "Donna, did you ever get your mammogram?" "No," I sheepishly confessed. "Well, I just scheduled my routine check," she replied. "Why don't you go with me?" I said, "Great! Just give me the date, time, and place." I was relieved that I was finally going to do something I had been meaning to do for so long.

A week and a half after my mammogram, I picked up my mail and opened a letter informing me that my mammogram results were abnormal! I immediately began calling on my network for information, support, comfort, and strength. I knew some people who had been through similar experiences. Others were family and friends whom I always include in my life. And I wanted to talk to some people because I value their thoughts and prayers. I called people I hadn't talked to in a while, people others recommended that I talk to, people who are near and dear to me. I was gathering my network of support around me.

The following week I was still reaching out to my network when I received a phone call from a woman I had met through networking. Barbie Adams works in academic affairs at The University of Texas M.D. Anderson Cancer Center. Over a six-month period, we had begun to develop a personal friendship as well as a professional connection. When she called, I told her my news. She gently expressed her concern and care. However, she also strongly asked me to keep her informed and to consider M.D. Anderson if any testing or treatment was necessary.

29

The first doctor recommended surgery, and I was waiting for another opinion when I received a message that Barbie had arranged to have my films seen by several doctors at M.D. Anderson. As they were being reviewed, I anxiously waited in her office. They suggested an ultrasound, and I scheduled one the following week. I had a sense of relief, a feeling that I was getting good information and taking steps in the right direction with the support of someone I knew who was competent and who cared. When the ultrasound showed a cluster of benign cysts, I went home with a new appreciation of life, the medical system, and my friends. I had been introduced to Barbie as a professional contact for my business and yet she became a valuable resource in my personal life.

CONNECTIONS TO COUNT ON

During the two-week period following my mammogram, I saw a cartoon that now hangs above my desk. It is a "Ziggy" cartoon, where Ziggy has climbed to the top of the mountain to ask the wise sage the meaning of life. The sage says to Ziggy, "Life? Why life is just one darn thing after another. I thought everyone knew that!"

So what can we count on in life? That life is just one darn thing after another? We can count on our network of support to be there for us no matter what circumstances and situations we have to face. Develop a lifetime network, a network of friends, family, and associates that you can count on and call on for support no matter what "darn thing" comes your way.

Times and Ways Your Network Can Be There for You:

☑ When you are looking for a new job opportunity

☑ When you are moving to a new city

☑ When you are faced with business challenges

☑ When you are looking for a great spot for a getaway weekend

☑ When you are dealing with a loss and need lots of emotional support

☑ When you are expanding your business into other cities

☑ When you are faced with health questions or concerns

☑ When you need to talk to someone

☑ When you want to be inspired

☑ When you want a mental boost or jump start

☑ When you want to brainstorm new ideas

☑ When you want validation and feedback regarding your thoughts

☑ When you are starting a business

☑ When you are building a business

☑ When you are hiring

☑ When you are looking for a new vendor or supplier of a particular product or service

31

Some people wait until things get really tough before they reach out to their network. Some people don't want to let others know when things are really tough, so they only network regarding impersonal and positive matters. As Susan Jeffers says in *Dare to Connect*, "It is through our humanness, not our perfection, that the poignant bonds of connection are finally formed." The true power of networking is universal. It applies to the ups as well as the downs of life. What good is a network if you do not use it to get over the hurdles? What good is a network if you do not give it the opportunity to respond to both the difficulties and the opportunities that come your way? You never know what needs or opportunities you will have today, tomorrow, next week, or in the years to come. However, you can know that you will always have a support system. Don't abandon or neglect your network when things are going well. Don't wait until there's a crisis before you reach out for support. Your relationships will deepen as you share your ups and downs with one another. Build a lifetime network and it will support you for life.

Build a Network You Can Count On

Answer the following questions to further develop a network you can count on:

How has my network supported me during a difficult time?

How has my network supported me in an unexpected way?

Who among my personal friends have supported me professionally?

Who among my professional contacts have become personal friends?

Who do I call on for comfort?

Who would I feel most comfortable calling on in a crisis situation?

What areas of my life are difficult for me to share with my network?

What am I willing to do differently to include my support system even more?

P A R T

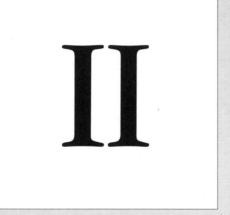

II

12 POWER PRINCIPLES
OF NETWORKING

CHAPTER FOUR

THE POWER OF GIVING

66 **W***e make a life by what we give.* *99*

—Winston Churchill

NETWORKING IS A TWO-WAY STREET. It is about creating a flow of mutual support between you and the other people in your life. One way to get that flow going is to give to people. It is an inherent human tendency to want to give back when one is given to. Giving of your time, energy, information, and contacts is one way to initiate networking relationships with people.

The concept that relates to the power of giving is what I call the "boomerang effect." What's the guarantee of the boomerang? It will come back, of course! However, you do have to take the initiative to step out and throw the boomerang just as you have to take the initiative with your network to give, participate, contribute, and ask for and offer support. Give, participate, contribute, and then watch. Be very aware. Opportunities will come your way, but you have to see and catch them or they will pass you by.

In his book *Flow,* psychologist Mihaly Csikszentmihalyi tells the story of Mehdi Fakharzadeh, Metropolitan Life Insurance Company's top agent, whose focus in life was helping people. Mehdi was contacted by one of his clients who wanted to file a claim. The client had suffered a heart attack and Mehdi knew that he had no prospect of selling him any additional insurance. He went to see the client and filled out the claim form for him. While talking with him, he learned that the client had policies with several other firms as well. So Mehdi took it upon himself to get the claim forms from the other agencies, fill them out, send them in, and follow up to make sure the refunds came through.

Many agents would have been focused on their goal of selling more policies and would have just handled their form with the client and gone on their way. The client appreciated Mehdi's support and wanted to pay him for his help, but Mehdi politely declined. A few days later, he received in the mail a list of twenty-one of the man's closest friends and relatives, with names, dates of birth, number of children, and other useful information, complete with a personal introduction to each. Mehdi reportedly sold millions of dollars of insurance to the people on this list.

Giving is a powerful way to activate your network. Even when there seems to be nothing in it for you, the satisfaction generated is tremendous. And it sets things in motion. People will realize that as a giver you are a valuable networking resource. For example, immediately after hearing my program "The Ten Commandments of Networking," Pippa Wiley, an agent with Farmers Insurance in Houston, recommended that I call the coordinator of the Farmers Insurance Regional Conference. She handed me her business card with the name and phone number of the contact person. I called, indicating that Pippa had referred me, and was eventually selected to speak at the conference.

Pippa is a giver! She has developed a focus that involves being aware of people and offering information and referrals without even being asked. She has trained herself to be proactive in her networking approach. Many people who have an abundance of ideas and contacts to offer have not trained themselves to share the vast resources they have in their network. You can learn to be a proactive giver.

As you learn to master the power of giving, remember to think of networking in terms of the big picture: even though you may give a lot to one person, the return may come back to you from someone else. You don't have to worry about keeping score. Simply trust the process and make sure that you are doing your part to give.

Develop a Giving Attitude and Approach

Answer the following questions to more fully develop a giving approach with your network:

In what ways could I be more giving and supportive?

In which personal relationships could I be more giving?

In which professional relationships could I be more giving?

Who will I call and ask, "What do you need?" and "How can I help?"

R E M I N D E R S

- *The more you give, participate, and contribute, the more value and satisfaction you receive.*
- *The "boomerang effect" of networking guarantees that opportunities will come your way once you take the initiative.*
- *Giving is a powerful way to activate your network.*

THE POWER OF INTERDEPENDENCE

" Interdependence is and ought to be as much the ideal of man as self-sufficiency. Man is a social being. "

—Mahatma Gandhi

T HE POWER OF INTERDEPENDENCE, as described by Stephen Covey in *The 7 Habits of Highly Successful People,* allows people to "combine their efforts with the efforts of others to achieve their greatest success." Covey describes interdependence as "a far more mature, more advanced concept" than independence. "As an interdependent person," Covey says, "I have the opportunity to share myself deeply, meaningfully, with others, and I have access to the vast resources and potential of other human beings."

Your attitude is as important as your skills in the networking process. And the attitude that gets in the way of networking is "I can do it on my own." In this mindset, you think that you are supposed to know everything, be able to do everything well, and do it on your own, never needing anyone's help. This is referred to as the "Lone Ranger mentality" in my book *Power Networking: 55 Secrets for Personal and Professional Success,* coauthored with Sandy Vilas. This mindset keeps people isolated, unavailable, and burdened with having to do everything on their own. The attitude of independence is prevalent in our society, and it will not go away on its own. However, you can make it go away when you begin to replace it with thoughts and ideas that create a new mentality, the mentality of interdependence.

With the interdependent mentality, people work together as independent people who each day do their part; by making sure everyone contributes, a larger goal is accomplished than could be achieved by any one person alone. It is only through the support of many people that you are able to do what you do. Take, for example, something as common as traveling. Many people are involved in making it possible to travel from Houston to San Jose to Vancouver and back through Phoenix to Houston. Many people would be involved even if it were just a matter of flying from Houston to Dallas and back. They include the travel agent, the airline mechanics, the baggage handlers, the pilots, flight attendants, air traffic controllers, parking attendants, and on and on. Each person contributes to the overall success of millions of people getting to their desired destination every day.

Think about your accomplishments. No matter what it took for you to achieve some accomplishment, other people were involved. For example, let's say that one of your accomplishments is having run in a marathon. Certainly you were the one who had to train and run those twenty-six miles. Yet could there have been a marathon without the sponsors, the police who set up the blockades, the people who monitored the time, those who handed you water along the way, and those who helped you train or supported you by encouraging you to take the time to train? This is the case with any accomplishment— many people are involved in many different ways. Realizing that others are involved in your success does not take away from your personal sense of accomplishment. Seeing how the synergy and interdependence of their support helps you can actually enhance your sense of personal fulfillment.

Debbie Golden had to think and move fast and use her networking skills when she was without work and needed a job quickly. When she heard about a job at the local college that fit her credentials, she decided to take her résumé in rather than mail it. While she was there, she talked to the director of the department. She asked who else in the college she should talk to and was directed to the controller's office, where she had another interview. She called to follow up and was scheduled for her third interview with the vice president the following week. Then, at a friend's house one evening, she casually mentioned her upcoming interview and one of the people there recommended that Debbie contact a friend of his who worked at the college. She called this friend of a friend and scheduled an appointment on the same day as her next interview.

Debbie's meeting with her friend's friend went very well, which she felt was due partly to their mutual acquaintance. When she left this meeting to go across campus to her interview, the new friend called to let the person who was interviewing her know that Debbie was on her way. Debbie felt as if she was being given another dose of special attention. Two days later she was offered the position. She credits her interdependent mindset and networking skills for helping her get so many interviews in such a short period of time.

BEWARE OF THE "I CAN DO IT ON MY OWN" MINDSET

When you are in need of information, support, or ideas, do you ask for what you want or do you try to figure things out for yourself? I recall a time when I was so focused on my business that I let months go by without doing other things I enjoy, like dancing, going for walks, and playing tennis. In spite of my very strong desire to maintain a positive balance in my life, I consistently allowed other things to take precedence. So I decided to ask for help and I started telling people about my desire to play tennis, go for walks, and dance. During the goal-setting portion of one of my training sessions, I talked about the difficulty I had encountered in making some seemingly simple changes in my life-style. I did this in front of a group of approximately sixty people and at the break two people came up to the front of the room with their daily planners. One of them said, "Okay, I walk in the park three time a week. Why don't you meet me there next week? How about Wednesday at 5:00 P.M.?" The other said, "I love to play tennis. When are you available?" It was a relief to be supported in making these life-style changes. When we don't do something we want to do, it is not necessarily because the desire is not there. Instead, we may need to realize the power of our habits and routines and call on our support system. Think about ways in which you can use your support system to help you make changes and implement the new behaviors and actions that will support you in achieving a healthy, happy, balanced life.

Steps for Developing the Power of Interdependence:

1. Give up thinking you have to be an expert about everything.
2. Notice when you are trying to handle things all by yourself.
3. Let people know you do not have all the answers.
4. Be vulnerable and ask for help from clients, management, associates, friends, and family.
5. Utilize the support of others.
6. Be a team player. Share tips, ideas, and information that work for you with others.
7. Accept and express appreciation for the support and contribution of others. Be aware of and fully acknowledge the people in your life who contribute to your success.
8. Discover the goals and needs of the people in your network so that you can support them.

DEVELOPING YOUR INTERDEPENDENCE

The "I can do it on my own" mentality limits your outreach and effectiveness as a networker. You may have allowed

 **Identify Your "I Can Do It on My Own" Mindset**

List examples of how you get caught up in the "I can do it on my own" mentality. This will help you to become more aware of how you may have been operating this way unconsciously. Through this awareness, you can begin to change your mindset.

Examples of this mindset in my personal life:

Examples of this mindset in my professional life:

I now see that I could do the following things differently:

yourself to be caught in this mentality by going along with this idea until it seemed true. Yet the truth resides in the statements that represent your interdependent mentality. You are ultimately in charge of your thoughts. You must retrain yourself to think in a positive manner about interdependence. Your new interdependent mentality will enhance your life, your business, and your career.

Move from Independence to Interdependence

"They probably don't have time to . . ." or "They wouldn't want to . . ."

Don't decide for other people. Give them the information and the opportunity to decide if and how they can respond.

The Interdependent Mentality:

> *"I allow others to make their own decisions about time."*

> *"I respect people's time by being efficient and effective with my requests."*

> *"I call on people in a way that honors their time."*

"I don't need anyone's help" or "I can do this myself."

Networking is not a matter of "needing" help; rather, it is a matter of making the best use of the resources available and working smart.

The Interdependent Mentality:

> *"I can accomplish even more with the assistance of others."*

> *"I work efficiently and effectively with others."*

> *"I appreciate the opportunity to call on the expertise of others."*

"I know what needs to be done here."

Even though you may think you know what needs to be done, your contacts can be a valuable source of confirmation or new ideas. Being rigid can get in the way of learning new, improved ways to get something done.

45

The Interdependent Mentality:

"By asking for the ideas of others, I can determine the best course of action."

"I run my ideas by others to verify and check my thinking."

"I am open to considering the ideas of others."

"I don't want to bother people" or "I can't call her. She's too busy."

Most people feel flattered when someone calls to sincerely ask for help. People want to contribute, but we have to reach out, let them know what we need, and give them permission to get involved.

The Interdependent Mentality:

"I call on people in a way that honors their time, talents, and availability."

"I include people and give them the opportunity to contribute."

"I acknowledge others by asking and including them."

"I don't know them well enough to call them."

One way to get to know people is by calling on them.

The Interdependent Mentality:

"I will expand my network by calling on people."

"I am willing to be the one to initiate getting to know someone better."

"I get to know people by calling on them."

"People will think I'm (weak, needy, stupid, wimpy) if I approach them about this" or *"I should be smart enough to figure this out myself."*

Some people are concerned that others will view them as inadequate if they ask for help of any kind. Asking for help and learning from others has nothing to do with not being smart. If others can help you learn something more quickly, isn't it smart to ask them?

47

The Interdependent Mentality:

"I'm smart enough to include others."

"People will know I respect their opinion if I approach them about this."

"People will realize how determined I am to accomplish this when I approach them for assistance."

"I have no right to expect others to help me out."

Networking is about exploring, not expecting. It is about inquiring, not demanding.

The Interdependent Mentality:

"I trust people to respond as best they can to my requests."

"I make requests in a nondemanding manner."

"I network with no strings attached."

"They probably don't know anyone who could help me."

Don't prejudge. You never know for sure until you ask.

The Interdependent Mentality:

"I approach people with an attitude of openness and unlimited possibilities."

"Everyone has a lot of contacts and some of those contacts could be of value to me."

"I'll never know if I don't ask."

---

*"I don't want them to realize I need help with this"
or "I don't want them to know I don't know how to handle this."*

Don't judge yourself. People tend to think they ought to know how to do something even when they've never done it before. Learning is part of life and the desire to learn is a positive trait. You don't have to come from a place of "neediness" to ask for and accept help.

The Interdependent Mentality:

"The more I learn from others, the smarter I become."

"I must let people know what I need so that they can network with me."

"I feel good about allowing others to contribute to my success."

With awareness, practice, and persistence, the interdependent mentality will become easy and natural. No matter what your goals are for your business, your career, and your personal life, you will always know other people with information, experiences, and contacts who can help you reach those goals more quickly and with more ease, fun, and satisfaction. There is no need to reinvent the wheel. Develop an attitude and style of interdependence and you may be pleasantly surprised to find a whole new world of networking relationships and opportunities!

49

PAUSE Define Your Interdependent Mentality

From the examples above, list the statements that reflect the interdependent mentality you would like to develop.

R E M I N D E R S

- *Your power comes from your interdependence.*

- *Networking is about working smart to accomplish your goals quickly.*

- *Catch yourself when you think those "I can do this on my own" thoughts and instead reach out to your network!*

- *There is no need to reinvent the wheel when you have a vast support system available to call on.*

CHAPTER SIX

THE POWER OF QUALITY CONNECTIONS

*66 **W**e think of ourselves as individuals,*
but we are embedded in networks of relationships
that define and sustain us. 99

—Michael P. Nichols

YOU ALREADY HAVE A VAST NET-WORK; however, the strength of that network is directly related to the quality and strength of your relationships. Building strong connections with the people you know is the best way to build and grow your network. It is easy to get busy and take relationships for granted. Yet, just as a car must be maintained to run in top condition and plants must be nurtured to grow and blossom, relationships must be given care, attention, trust, and support. With strong, mutually supportive relationships in your network, your results and accomplishments will flourish.

Imagine that you have a fruit tree. Obviously, what you want to do is pick the fruit off the tree and eat it! But first, you have to remember to water the tree. If the tree gets no water, it will wither and have no blossoms and no fruit. However, if you remember that your priority is to water the tree, the rest becomes a natural process. The tree will grow and blossom, produce fruit, grow larger, and produce more fruit. Your network is the same. If you focus on nurturing, strengthening, and building the relationships around you, your network will grow and blossom and produce results, grow larger, and produce more results. It is very easy today to become focused on picking the fruit, or producing the result. However, you must remember that the priority is to water the tree, or strengthen the relationships. It is your relationships that lead to the results.

Now, once again, think about the analogy of watering the tree. It only takes little drops of water to make the tree grow big and strong. In relationships, the little things make a difference in building strong connections that are long-lasting. This is a reminder: Don't let those little things slide! In his book *Opening Closed Doors,* Richard Weylman says, "It's the cup of coffee you buy, it's the chocolate or cashews that you bring to the secretary, it's the thank you notes you send, it's asking about the children, it's finding out about how the wife or husband is doing, it's telling someone you're going to pray for them and then letting them know you have; it's all these things that make a difference . . . particularly in relation to how you build a mutually rewarding, long-term relationship. . . . We know that people are less brand-loyal than ever before—they have become people-loyal instead."

Another analogy regarding networking and relationships is with computer networking. With computer networking, you hook up two or more computers with a common communication link so they can share information back and forth and access the same data. It's the same thing with people networking. Your *people network* consists of people who are connected, and the communication link is their relationships. The stronger the relationships, the more information is naturally passed back and forth throughout the network.

You have a vast network. Some of the links are very strong. Some, however, may be weak and rusty. Now is the time to become more aware of your network and clean up all those communication lines and links so that you can network with all the people in your life in an easy, natural, and consistent manner.

You can probably think of some people you could call on anytime, anywhere, for anything, who would always be there for you. They provide unconditional support. You have strong, quality relationships in your life. You may think those relationships are special and just "happened"! But if you think back over a period of time, you can probably recall some of the little things that contributed to the specialness of your relationships with those people—the way you included them, the way they responded to your need, the way you were vulnerable with them, the time you asked them for help. You can have a network full of relationships with that "special" quality of unconditional support.

Ways to Honor Your Relationships:

☑ Be courteous.

☑ Speak words of appreciation.

☑ Ask about people's children, family, interests, and hobbies.

☑ Take time to listen.

☑ Include people in your projects and activities.

☑ Notice and celebrate others' accomplishments.

☑ Offer support and friendship.

☑ Give encouragement to others freely.

☑ Stay in touch through calls, notes, getting together.

☑ Remember special occasions.

"IF YOU NEED ME, I'LL BE THERE"

My friend Doug is a great example of the way a high level of friendship contributes to a strong network and a fulfilling life. He has a very strong network of people who seem to have an unspoken creed: "If you need me, I'll be there." Doug and his friend Jerry grew up together and have stayed in touch through the years. They've known each other in good times and bad. If Jerry needs something done around his home, Doug responds automatically with the information, the supplies, or the right people to get the job done. He is simply glad to be of service to his friend. At the same time, if Doug has a health question, Jerry is there on the phone at any time of the day or night to answer his questions, offer suggestions, and provide assistance. I've seen this happen with no mention of money, no mention of fees, no concern about anything other than being friends who care about each other and are there for each other. Their work does not depend on their doing business with each other. Their businesses depend on the many client and vendor relationships they have carefully built over the years. They appear to be glad to have the opportunity to give of their friendship.

I seem to always be asking advice of my computer friends, Byron, Randon, and Amy, who support me so graciously with my questions and calls for help. I use the computer a lot and I love learning how to use it more efficiently and effectively. Amy, one of my computer angels, used to work for me and we have stayed in touch as friends for years. She is now the business manager for an optical company. She is very knowledgeable about the computer and is excellent at editing and proofreading. Over the last ten years, she has consistently been very gracious and patient with my computer questions and has also reviewed my articles and book manuscripts for me. She has come to my office and spent hours working with me to get a new computer program working. I sometimes worry about her giving so much to me so generously. When I ask her about it, she assures me that I give to her in many ways. I certainly look for ways to be of mutual support. Recently, I was pleased to have the opportunity to sit down with Amy and help guide her in developing a business and marketing plan for a new venture she is launching. It didn't seem like much to me. Yet for her it may not seem like much to answer my computer questions. I appreciate having friends in my network, like Amy, who trust that everything balances out over time.

55

GETTING TO KNOW YOU

A relationship is strengthened through getting to know the other person, sharing information, and offering mutual support. The mistake we sometimes make is to think we already know people rather than taking the time to get to know them better. In one of my training sessions, people are matched with a different person in the training each week for a get-acquainted meeting. They may have breakfast or lunch together but the main thing is to listen, gather information, and get to know each other. I always get the same feedback at the end of the eight-week training: "I probably wouldn't have reached out to these people on my own and yet with *every person* I met we found something we had in common and some way we could be of support to one another." When you take the time to listen and get to know someone, you will almost always find some basis for relating and networking.

We also use the concept of the get-acquainted meeting in our business breakfast club, The Windsor Club. At each meeting we're given a list that matches each club member with another member. Even though we might think that we already know each other, the get-acquainted meetings serve to keep us in touch with each other, network consistently, and deepen our relationships.

Business lunches can be powerful get-acquainted meetings. Sometimes that personal meeting with a prospect or client can solidify an important business relationship. It may seem as if the purpose of the business lunch is to eat or conduct business, but it's not; the purpose is to get to know each other better and thus build a relationship. Rhonda Abrams, writer for Gannett News Service, gives some tips in her article "Doing Lunch More Than Just Having a Meal." "'Doing lunch' successfully is a skill that, with practice and training, can be developed just like other business skills," she says. "This is not a two-way street. You should be more interested in your client than he will be with you. Therefore the most important skill is listening." Learn how to ask questions without making it seem like an interview and ask some questions about other people's personal life so that you are not totally focused on business.

AUSE Who Are the Five Most Well-Connected People You Know?

By consciously building relationships with people who know people, you are multiplying your reach. List five people you know who are well connected and identify what you will do to strengthen your relationship with each of them. For each person, include the following information:

How can I be a valuable resource for this person?

How can this person be a valuable resource for me?

What will I do to strengthen this relationship?

When they ask about you, respond in a friendly, informative, and easy manner, while focusing primarily on areas you have in common with one another.

HOW TO GET ACQUAINTED

Following are some guidelines for get-acquainted meetings.

Ask Questions

Find out about the other person by asking questions that encourage the person to talk about his or her life and business:

"I would like to understand your business better."

"What do you love most about what you do?"

"How did you happen to get into (this business, this type of work)?"

"What brought you to (New York, Chicago, . . .)?"

Ask questions that help you develop a sense of rapport and relationship with the other person. You want to get to know the person better and at the same time learn more about his or her business and needs so that you will know how you can be of support. Through good conversational skills, you will almost always be able to develop a rapport that leads to some ways to network and be of support.

Focus on Being a Resource

Listen for opportunities to offer ideas or contacts that can provide information, expertise, or assistance to the other

 Grow Your Relationships

With a little attention you can strengthen your network tremendously. Ask yourself:

Which personal relationships do I want to strengthen?

Which client relationships do I want to strengthen? (Include your top ten clients.)

Which relationships serve as valuable centers of influence and key sources of referrals?

Which relationships are important for my career network?

person. Think about the people you know who might be good contacts for the person as a prospect, friend, associate, or resource. Even when you cannot immediately respond as a resource, make a mental note of the things you are learning about the person.

Practice Active Listening

Use active listening to make sure that you understand and to ensure that the other person feels heard. Lead-in phrases for active listening include:

> *"Are you saying...?"*
>
> *"So what you want is...?"*
>
> *"What I think I hear you saying is..."*
>
> *"If I could give you a contact with..., would that address what you're looking for?"*
>
> *"If I understand you correctly, what you've identified as your most immediate need is..."*

Let People Know Your Needs

Be willing to let the other person get to know you better. Be a little vulnerable. Let him or her know what you need, what you want, what is working well, and what type of help would be of support.

Thank the Other Person

Acknowledge the other person for what you appreciate: her or his time, attention, honesty, openness, perceptiveness, persistence, patience, information, contacts, and so on.

Taking the time to get to know people can lead to opportunities you never realized were available. Don't ever think you already know everything there is to know about someone. Be interested. Be open to new possibilities. See what you might learn about the other person that you didn't already know. Be open to a new level of relationship that will continue to be a source of referrals, support, contacts, and satisfaction.

People do business with people they like. Most people base their buying decisions on some level of trust, rapport, and relationship. People will typically ask all about your background, client list, pricing, service, and other business factors, but, even though all of that information is valuable and important, they often respond most strongly to their gut instinct. A sense of rapport and trust is what will cause people to do business with you, stay on as clients, refer to you, hire you, and network with you. Strong relationships will be a natural source of referrals, support, and contacts. The strength of your contacts is the source of an ever-expanding base of lifelong relationships.

R E M I N D E R S

- *Never underestimate the power of your contacts.*

- *Your network will naturally grow and blossom as you strengthen and nurture your relationships.*

- *People do business with those they know and trust.*

- *Strong relationships lead to powerful results.*

- *Nurturing your relationships ensures a lifetime of networking.*

THE POWER OF PRAISE

"Kind words can be short and easy to speak, but their echoes are truly endless."

—Mother Teresa

AN ATTITUDE OF GRATITUDE provides the nourishment for a network that will naturally grow and blossom. Do you freely express gratitude and appreciation to your friends, family, and associates? It is easy to think, "Oh, she knows I appreciate her," or "He knows I love him," or "She knows she did well on that project." Don't let those thoughts get in the way of expressing your appreciation. Be generous, spontaneous, and sincere in passing along to others your thoughts of gratitude and appreciation.

Dr. Shad Helmstetter, in his book *What to Say When You Talk to Yourself,* cites the importance of giving positive feedback to ourselves and others. "During the first eighteen years of our lives," he says, "if we grew up in fairly average, reasonably positive homes, we were told 'No!' or what we could not do, more than 148,000 times." That "no" could be in the form: "You can't do that," "Not now," "Don't be ridiculous," "You might as well not try," or "Don't be silly."

During that same eighteen years, we may receive positive feedback only a few times. This is a staggering and alarming statistic. "Whatever the number," Helmstetter says, "for most of us the 'yes's' we received simply didn't balance out the 'no's.'"

With that in mind, praise is not just a good idea; it is vital to counteract all of that negative feedback, and we are way behind. Most people do not get or give enough positive reinforcement. They are hungry for appreciation and positive strokes. Think about all the people who support you personally and professionally. Praise is the act of giving positive and sincere feedback and reinforcement to those people. And you can't just tell people once that you appreciate them. Appreciation and caring must be expressed in a spontaneous, sincere, and consistent manner. Acknowledge the people around you, give them words of nourishment, and watch them grow and blossom.

There are two main ways to regularly acknowledge people in your network: (1) by speaking to them, either in person or over the phone, and (2) by sending them notes.

SPEAKING WORDS OF PRAISE

As Kenneth Blanchard says in his best-seller *The One Minute Manager,* "Catch people doing things right." And let them know that you notice and appreciate what they are "doing right." Blanchard recommends that you praise people immediately. So, at the end of your phone conversations, thank people for their call, their time, their feedback. At the end of company or family meetings, take the last few moments as a time for acknowledgments, when anyone can verbally express appreciation to anyone else in the meeting. Be on the lookout to catch people doing things right and you will find yourself acknowledging people all around you.

SENDING NOTES

It is often the little things in life that touch us, and sending personal handwritten notes is one of those seemingly little

TIPS ON VERBAL ACKNOWLEDGMENTS

1. Give acknowledgments to people directly. Look them in the eye. Make sure you've got their attention. Don't mumble or act as if your comment is unimportant. Say it with substance:

   "John, I appreciate the way you . . ."

2. Be specific. When you make a generic acknowledgment, some people will discount it by saying to themselves, "Oh, she says that to everyone" or "He always says that." Rather than making broad or general statements, be direct about what it is you appreciate about others. This more personal approach conveys sincerity and warmth and is more likely to get their attention:

   "Jane, I happened to notice how you responded to that customer. I like the way you listened and addressed her concern so that she felt taken care of."

3. Acknowledge people for what they do as well as for the characteristics or qualities they exhibit. Give positive feedback regarding their values, strengths, and inherent abilities as well as the way they are using those strengths and skills to get things done:

   "Congratulations on your new venture. I admire your courage in stepping out on your own."

   "Thanks for referring David to me. We hit it off right away and I look forward to working with his firm. I appreciate having you as a powerful resource in my life."

   "Thanks for your hospitality. I thoroughly enjoyed my visit. You are a gracious host."

---

things that means a lot. A handwritten note conveys the personal touch that we often yearn for in our society. Sending notes helps us to stay in touch with people. It also helps us to stay uplifted, focused, and on track by reminding us to maintain an attitude of gratitude. Notes are not just for the people receiving them; it is important for us to express the gratitude and appreciation that we feel. Writing a note takes very little time or energy but it has long-lasting effects.

Tom Peters, in his book *The Pursuit of Wow!* says, "The power of a thank you...is hard—make that impossible—to beat." What about thank-you phone calls? Phone calls are okay but, as Peters says, "Lifting up a phone is pretty easy. Writing a note demonstrates a level of effort and is permanent. Typed or handwritten? Handwritten by a country mile. A two-line largely unreadable scrawl beats a page-and-a-half on the laser printer."

Fred Bauer touches on how a note can "brighten a day, motivate a co-worker and sometimes change a life," in his article "The Power of a Note," published in *Reader's Digest* magazine. The drawback with phone calls is that they don't last, while a note is a written record that gives more importance to our words of appreciation and "can be read more than once, savored and treasured." Bauer tells how the former Ford chairman, Donald Petersen, sent a positive message to some of his associates every day. Petersen believed that the "most important ten minutes of your day are those you spend doing something to boost the people who work for you. Too often people we genuinely like have no idea how we feel about them. We forget that human beings need positive reinforcement—in fact, we thrive on it!"

According to Bauer, it takes "only unselfish eyes and a willingness to express our appreciation" to become proficient at sending notes that lift the spirit and warm the heart. He recommends four "S's" of note writing. A note should be:

1. *Sincere*—Let it come from the heart.

2. *Short*—It should be anywhere from one to three sentences, and no more than three.

3. *Specific*—Key in on something regarding that person. Notice the difference in a note that says, "Good speech!" versus the power that comes across with the more specific "Great story in your speech about Joe Smith's marketing strategy."

4. *Spontaneous*—The freshness and enthusiasm that are conveyed when we express what we feel in the moment have a long-lasting effect.

Send Notes Frequently That Say:

☑ Thanks for your support.

☑ Thanks for your friendship.

☑ Thanks for the referral.

☑ Thanks for the ideas you shared with me.

☑ Thanks for your interest in our firm.

☑ Thanks for the words of encouragement.

☑ Thanks for the opportunity to learn more about your business.

☑ Thank you for your confidence in me.

☑ Thanks for sending that article on . . .

☑ Thanks for thinking of me.

☑ Thank you for the opportunity to do business with you.

☑ You are one of my favorite clients. Thanks for being so great to work with.

☑ Thanks for the opportunity to meet with you.

☑ Thanks for taking the time to . . .

☑ Thanks for staying in touch.

SPECIAL THANKS

There are times when you will feel a desire to send more than a note; your praise is so meaningful or the acknowledgment so important that you want to send a gift. Some of the most cherished gifts are not necessarily the largest, most expensive, or most extravagant. Often they are the ones that are "special" in their thoughtfulness.

Truly Memorable Gifts

• Tickets to the person's favorite play or sporting event

- A mounted and framed business card (for someone starting his or her own business)

- A cartoon that has some special meaning or significance to the person

- A book on a topic that is of special interest

- A framed announcement or business article about someone's business

- An arrangement of the person's favorite flowers

- A heart-shaped box filled with handwritten words of inspiration

Other Gift Ideas

- Personalized Post-it Notes
- A letter opener
- A paperweight
- Note cards
- A business card holder
- A magazine subscription
- A plant
- A gift basket
- An audiotape
- A fruit basket
- A calendar
- A pen and pencil set

It can be helpful to have some gift ideas ready and to know where to find the kind of present that you like to give. Janet Shorr is the owner of a gift basket company called "Instead Of." We initially met through a professional organization. I have visited her store and ordered gift baskets from her. We have been to lunch together. I have even been the happy recipient of her baskets. By knowing her and being familiar with her baskets, it's easy for me to call, let her know what I have in mind, order a gift, and have it delivered.

I conducted an all-day training program on networking for the partners and attorneys of a Houston law firm. During the afternoon session, "How to Make Requests of Your Network," I placed them in groups of six and they made requests of one another. Every person made at least two requests of his or her group. As I walked around among the groups, one of the attorneys asked the group for information on how the firm could get articles published in newspapers and magazines as a way to create more visibility. I responded by giving him the name and phone number of Phil Morabito, president of Pierpont Communications, a Houston-based public relations firm. Phil immediately came to mind because I knew of several people who had gotten articles published in local and national publications through his efforts.

A few months later, I had forgotten about the referral when I got a phone message from Phil saying thanks. They had just finalized an agreement to do public relations work for the law firm. I was thrilled. I felt that both of them would be pleased with the results, and it was a nice feeling to have helped their two companies connect with one another. I felt sufficiently thanked by Phil's call, but the next day I was pleasantly surprised to receive a flower arrangement from Pierpont Communications. A nice touch! Phil's company was honored the last two years as one of the fastest-growing companies in Houston. His awareness of the value of acknowledging people for their support is probably one of the factors that contributes to his exceptional and consistent success.

Make it easy on yourself. Find a gift basket shop, a florist, a frame shop, and a gift store where you know the people and they know you. Set up an account with them so that it is easy to call and order a gift. Often people have good intentions about sending a note or a gift, and yet the majority of the time it never happens. Develop relationships with vendors who can help you and set up an easy way to follow through on your

 Your Acknowledgment List

List the people you would like to acknowledge by writing a note. Include the following categories: family, friends, clients, prospects, co-workers, employees and employers, and associates, as well as other people such as neighbors, former employers, and community leaders.

thought. You've heard that it's the thought that counts; in this case, it's following through on the thought that counts!

It seems that the more I notice and acknowledge the people around me for what they are doing, the more I feel good and appreciative in general. And when I feel appreciative, I am more likely to approach people in a positive and gracious manner; this results in more effective and satisfying networking interactions.

 Set Up Your Gift-Giving System

Establish a system for giving gifts that will allow you to do it effortlessly. Identify the following information:

What sources would I like to use for gift-giving purposes?

What gifts and notes have I received that have meant a lot to me?

69

REMINDERS

- *Be on the lookout—there is always something to acknowledge people for.*

- *Be generous, spontaneous, and sincere with your acknowledgments.*

- *You can never overacknowledge as long as you are sincere and the acknowledgment is given with no strings attached!*

- *A thoughtful person is a remembered person.*

THE POWER OF
STAYING IN TOUCH

*❝**O**ne of the greatest gifts you can give to anyone is the gift of your attention.*❞

—Jim Rohn

EVERYONE HAS A VAST NETWORK, and yet some people's networks are largely dormant. It is not enough just to have a network. You must cultivate your network for growth, action, and interactions. It's important not only to know people, but to stay in touch with them. Staying connected enhances communication and increases networking.

When I conduct trainings for people who are in job transition, I routinely hear comments such as "I sure wish I had been networking all along" or "I wish I had stayed in touch with..." or "I wish I had realized the importance of networking before this downsizing happened." Staying in touch with people is like the little drops of water that make the trees grow and blossom: it keeps our relationships close and connected. There have been many times when I have wished that I had learned the value and importance of networking earlier in my life. I've lost contact with some people I did not stay in touch with and I don't know how to find them anymore. Staying in touch keeps us aware, keeps us available, and keeps us networking with one another.

"I'VE BEEN MEANING TO CALL"

I received a phone call a couple of months ago that reminded me of the importance of staying in touch. I answered the phone in my office one day: "Hi, this is Donna!" "Donna, hi, this is Karl Anthony." My response was a scream of surprise and delight: "Karl Anthony, how are you? *Where* are you? How are you doing?" I had not talked to Karl in at least seven years and yet I had thought of him many times. He is one of those friends for whom I have a warm place in my heart, but over time, with new addresses and new careers, we had lost contact.

We had some wonderful, fond memories of participating in the same church activities and musical programs. Karl is an excellent singer and musician who is especially gifted in working with young people and who takes groups of teenagers to Russia and China. He said he was reading a magazine on the plane coming back from one of his trips when he saw a photo of me alongside an article I had written on networking. A few days after he arrived back home, he talked to a mutual friend of ours, Chaka, whom I had just visited in Austin, Texas. She mentioned that I had been over for the weekend, and Karl mentioned that he had seen my article. Chaka gave him my number and encouraged him to call, and he did!

It was a treat to hear from Karl, to reconnect, to hear about his recent wedding and the wonderful work he is doing with his music. We discovered that we both belong to the National Speakers Association and talked about the possibility of getting together at one of the association's regional or national conventions.

Why, when Karl's call was so wonderful, is it still hard sometimes to pick up the phone and call someone I want to reconnect with? It may be difficult because I think that I "should have" called sooner. Or I may feel uncomfortable about some aspect of my life that didn't turn out the way I thought it would. Reconnecting would mean catching up on what has and hasn't happened. I may be afraid that the other person won't even remember me. I even may feel uncomfortable to be calling with no purpose, just to say hello. Will it be awkward? What will I say? What will the other person say?

Every time I make a call and have a good experience, I am more encouraged to call someone else. Even though I am calling strictly to reconnect with people, the networking happens as a natural part of the conversation. For example, when I ask, "Tell me what you're doing!" or "How's your family?" or "Give me an update. What's happening?" the people I'm calling respond with information. The information might be something that's of interest to me or something about which I can offer support. Or it might be of value to someone else I know. And typically, after telling me what's going on in their lives, they will come back and inquire about mine. I get an update on what they are doing while they hear the same from me. The conversation is a natural source for networking. Yet someone must be willing to initiate the conversation.

PEOPLE ARE ONLY A PHONE CALL AWAY

To help me stay in touch with my network, I have focused on developing the habit of calling at least one person a week I haven't talked with in a long time. Imagine if every week for the rest of your life you made just one phone call to someone you hadn't talked to in a while. Imagine what your network would be like over your lifetime with this kind of attention— how alive, connected, and available it would be. And imagine, with your connections current, how easy it would be to call and ask for support or assistance, because the relationships have been honored and nurtured along the way.

Can you recall a time when you got a call from someone you hadn't talked with in a long time? It probably didn't take much to get back into your relationship. In fact, I often have people say that it was almost as if no time had passed. Almost everyone has thought about calling someone and yet not followed through on that thought. So don't let feeling bad or guilty get in the way of calling. Instead, be the one who is willing to do something about it now. The people you call will probably be glad that you had the gumption to pick up the phone and call. It's much easier to stay in touch with people than it is to track them down after a long period of time has passed.

When calling to reconnect with people, sometimes all you have to say is:

"Can you believe it's been ... years?"

"Do you remember the time we worked on the ... project together?"

"I was thinking about you because ..."

"I was talking to ... and I thought of you."

"I was thinking about my career and I thought about how you influenced me with ..."

Make reconnecting with your network a priority in your life. So what if you haven't talked to someone in quite a while? Calling now is better than waiting and then having the time be even longer.

SEVEN TYPES OF CALLS TO CULTIVATE YOUR NETWORK

Relationships have many levels and depths. You have best friends whom you talk to and see on a very regular basis, co-workers and family members you see on a daily basis, and top clients who require consistent attention. Other friends, acquaintances, and prospects can become even stronger links in your network as you cultivate connections with them. Following are descriptions of the types of calls you might make.

The "Reconnection" Call

The reconnection call is a call to someone you have not talked to in a while. It is made for the purpose of reconnecting, reestablishing the relationship, and getting an update on what the other person is doing. You can start out by acknowledging that it has been a long time, then expressing an interest in catching up. Even if it feels awkward at first, most of the time the relationship can be reestablished fairly quickly.

> *"Rodney, this is Gail Smith. We sang together in the Pasadena Choir at Strawberry Festival several years ago."*

> *"Cathy, this is Steve Jones. We used to work together at ABC Associates."*

> *"Mark, this is Stephanie Harper, used to be Stephanie Walters, from the Center for Community Action."*

> *"Carol, this is Bob Blanchard. I met you last fall at the Medical Professional Conference in Seattle."*

The "Follow-Through" Call

A "follow-through" call is made to follow up on a project or idea. The call may involve giving or asking for information, scheduling a meeting or appointment, or staying in touch about an opportunity.

> *"Hi, this is Jane, calling to follow up to schedule our meeting about next year's conference."*

> *"This is Harry. I wanted to touch base about the project we discussed last month."*

The "New Contact or Referral" Call

You make this call to either someone you have just met or someone you have not yet met who has been referred to you by someone you know. With a "new contact or referral" call, you are just getting to know each other. This is an opportunity to gather information to see if and how you can provide mutual support. With a referral call, obviously it is important to indicate up front who referred you. With calls to people you have just recently met, it is good to remind them of where you met.

> *"Hello, my name is Joan Smothers. I got your name and number from Jack Lawrence."*

> *"Hi, my name is Larry Harris. Margaret Evans recommended that I contact you about . . ."*

> *"Hi, this is Greg Marvin. I met you last week at the . . . and we talked about . . ."*

The "Thinking of You" Call

It is important with friends, clients, and associates to call occasionally for no particular reason other than to say hi and let them know that you are thinking of them. I sometimes hear complaints about insurance agents who make a sale and then are never heard from again. During the sales process, a great deal of interest is expressed in the prospect's financial future and security. Then, once the sale is made, that interest suddenly disappears. With no other contact, the automatic birthday card each year does not make people feel that the interest was sincere. There's nothing wrong with sending birthday cards. In fact, when some other contact takes place throughout the year, those birthday cards are really appreciated. But when the birthday card is the only contact, it comes across to many people as a mechanical technique. A "thinking of you" call is a simple way of keeping the communication lines open—no sales pitch, no request, no agenda, no expectations. Just "Hi, how are you? I was thinking of you and wanted to call."

> *"Hi, this is Bill. Just calling to say hi and find out how the book is coming along. Give me a call when you get a chance."*

> *"Hi, this is Martha. I haven't seen you in a while and have missed you. No real need to call back. Just wanted to say hi. Hope you're doing great!"*

"Hi, this is Joey. Just calling to check in and see how things are going!"

The "Asking for Support" Call

This call is made to request information, ideas, contacts, or support of some kind. The main thing is to be clear about what you want and how you think this person can be of help. Let people know what is special about them that caused you to call. The call is not only a request for something; it is also a form of research where you are gathering information and learning more about some topic. This type of call can provide value in the form of information, a recommendation, a referral, an appointment, words of encouragement, new ideas, or new opportunities.

"Hello, this is Frank Chandler. I'm looking for some information about day care centers in the area. I thought you might be able to help me."

"Hello, this is Mary Morrison. I wanted to find out who you would recommend I call about getting a new brochure designed for my company."

The "How Can I Help?" Call

You make this call to offer support and make yourself available as a resource. When you hear about a project or challenge that someone is facing, call. If you hear that someone is going through a job search, you can call and offer both ideas and moral support. You may have to ask some questions to find out what is really needed. However, just by calling you are showing that you care. Letting someone know that you are available can mean a lot. People often don't know what to ask for, but with good listening and asking skills, you may be able to find out enough to know what to offer. Support comes in many forms—a shoulder to cry on, an ear that listens, a word of encouragement, a piece of information, a hand to hold.

"Hi. This is George. I remember hearing you comment at breakfast last week that you were looking for information about . . . I wanted to let you know about . . ."

"Hi, this is Tom Carpenter. Roger told me you are looking for a position in . . . I wanted to see if I could be of help in any way."

"Hello, this is Karen. I'm so sorry to hear about your mother's illness. What do you need? How can I help?"

The "Developing Friendship" Call

Sometimes you meet someone and recognize an easy, natural rapport that leaves you wanting to get together with that person again. A "developing friendship" call is very similar to a "thinking of you" call, yet the focus is to create an opportunity for a personal or professional friendship to develop. You make the call to someone you feel an initial sense of connection or camaraderie with and want to get to know better.

"Hi. This is Charles Lawson. I enjoyed our brief visit last week and wanted to see about getting together for lunch."

"Hi. This is Gayle Bryan. I enjoyed working with you at the expo last month. Hope things are going well. I wanted to see if you would like to join me for a round of golf this weekend."

STAYING IN TOUCH PAYS OFF

As a young married couple, Sally and Butch Wilson joined with three other couples to start a dinner club. All of the couples were young, newly married, just starting their careers, and building their lives. A year later Butch and Sally were transferred from Illinois to Pennsylvania and then later to Texas.

AUSE Smiling and Dialing

List people to call for each of the seven types of calls: (1) the "reconnection" call, (2) the "follow-through" call, (3) the "new contact or referral" call, (4) the "thinking of you" call, (5) the "asking for support" call, (6) the "how can I help?" call, and (7) the "developing friendship" call.

Over the years, they stayed in touch with Mike and Mary Lynn McLintock, a couple from the dinner club. Sally admits that in the beginning it was primarily the McLintocks' initiative that kept them connected. But then, through the years, calls and notes were sent from both directions, and occasionally they would visit when a trip took them to one another's cities.

Twenty years after they first met, Mike called to say that he had been laid off and was looking for a position in advertising and public relations. He said he was calling all his friends and asking for information and contacts. Sally happened to be the one who talked with him when he called. Her first thought was to start reading the want ads to look for something that would be of interest to Mike. Then she remembered that Butch had recently mentioned that his firm was looking for an advertising manager. Butch called Mike. Mike interviewed and got the position and he and Mary Lynn moved to Texas.

The job turned out to be a perfect fit for Mike and he and Mary Lynn both said that it was one of the best moves they had ever made. They felt that a phone call to a friend from twenty years earlier was instrumental in their taking a step that gave Mike much greater potential in his career. These four people will probably be friends, and networking friends, for life. All it takes is some form of contact, some amount of communication, to keep your network accessible for life.

Regina Bruce, a financial consultant with Merrill Lynch, attended a networking training in Dallas and followed through on the idea of calling to reconnect with people. One of the people she called was a college friend with whom she had not talked in over a year. She and her friend had gone to the same college, worked at the same accounting firm for a while, and then gone in separate directions. She found out by making the call that her friend was moving back to Dallas. They talked over the phone and agreed to get together once the friend had moved. Regina's friend gave her two contacts that led to new accounts right away. A year later, one of the contacts led to a new portfolio in excess of one million dollars! And over a one-year period, Regina has gained seven new accounts totaling $1.7 million from that initial phone call—all because she followed through with the impulse to reconnect with a college friend.

When you do a good job of staying in touch, you are ensuring that your current network will be part of your future network, your lifetime network. Build your network for the future. Don't be shortsighted or get caught up in immediate gratification. Building a support system over a lifetime creates phenomenal results and an incredible sense of joy and fulfillment. If you have not been focused on staying in touch with people, take advantage of this new opportunity that can lead to a lifetime of opportunities.

81

REMINDERS

- *It is up to you to keep the communication lines open so that your networking happens in an easy, natural, and consistent manner.*

- *Your network is only a phone call away.*

- *Staying in touch with people keeps your network alive and active.*

CHAPTER NINE

THE POWER OF KNOWING YOU

When one is a stranger to oneself then one is estranged from others too. If one is out of touch with oneself, then one cannot touch others.

—Anne Morrow Lindbergh

SINCE YOU ARE THE CENTER OF your network, you must lay the foundation for a strong lifetime network by starting with yourself. Learn to take good care of yourself so that you can be available to the people in your network. Build a strong sense of self so that you will have the confidence to approach people in a positive, professional manner. Develop clarity about your personal purpose so that you can honor what is important to you in life, and clarity about your business and career mission that will help to keep you on track professionally. Keeping your goals in sharp focus will give you greater power in calling on your network for the information and resources that will help you fulfill your vision. You are the power source for your network to be an active, powerful support system that enriches your life.

THE POWER OF YOUR PURPOSE

What are you here for? What is important to you in life? What is life about for you? Answering these questions calls for introspection. It requires that you access a knowingness and wisdom that resides deep inside your heart and soul. David McNally, in *Even Eagles Need a Push,* states that finding the answer to the question, "What is your purpose in life?" is "the biggest single thing you can do to further your happiness." Take time periodically to reflect, look within, and maintain an appreciation for what is important in life.

Personal Purpose Statements:

> *"My personal purpose is to experience the adventure of life each day."*

> *"My personal purpose is to be respectful of all living creatures."*

> *"My personal purpose is to live a life of dignity and respect for myself and all of humankind."*

> *"My personal purpose is to experience my spiritual connection."*

> *"My personal purpose is to be a joyful spirit."*

Sometimes people find it very difficult to come up with a statement of personal purpose because they worry about having the "right" purpose. If that's so for you, insert the words "as I see it now" into your personal purpose sentence to ease your concern. You will continue to gain a deeper sense of your purpose as you grow through facing your own challenges and opportunities in life.

> *"My personal purpose as I see it now is to be a growing, contributing human being."*

> *"My personal purpose as I see it now is to enjoy life."*

> *"My personal purpose as I see it now is to love myself unconditionally."*

Create Your Personal Purpose Statement

Answer the following questions to help develop your personal purpose statement:

What would be the greatest expression of fulfillment for me with my life?

If there is any one thing I would like to be able to say about my life overall it would be that I . . .

How would I best define my personal purpose at this moment?

RECLAIMING YOUR GOALS

Goal setting can sometimes become a serious, guilt-producing process because of the times we have set goals that never were accomplished. Goal setting is best approached as a brainstorming session, an energizing, fun process. Don't judge yourself or set goals that you think you "should" have. Don't decide that something is impossible before you even write it down. Explore your thoughts, feelings, dreams. It may be time to refocus on a goal you previously gave up on or had to set aside because of other priorities. Write down everything you think you would like to do.

Staying aware of your goals in all areas of your life helps you to maintain a life of balance and to stay more aware of how to best call on your network for support. Often people forget to network regarding some of the "little things" in life. Whether you're considering a health question, a vacation idea, a hobby you've always wanted to pursue, a job opportunity, a purchase you want to make, or a new skill you want to develop, your network is a powerhouse of information and support.

THE GUIDING FORCE OF YOUR BUSINESS AND CAREER

A business or career mission statement provides focus and direction. It is the guiding statement for the fulfillment of your career goals and your business success. If you are a business owner, write your business mission statement. If you work for a company, then write either a job or career mission statement. The process of writing this statement requires that you crystallize your thoughts about what you want to accomplish through your work, in your profession, or with your business.

My friend, image consultant Katherine Ashby, developed her mission statement when she started her business: "The purpose of my business is to use my ability to recognize and call forth the inherent beauty of the individual through their dress so they can have an impressive self-presentation that moves them forward in realizing their intentions and fully expressing who they are becoming." She had it written in beautiful calligraphy and framed. It was placed on the wall of

87

 This Is Your Life — A Goals Worksheet

List three short-term and long-term goals for each of the six areas of your life: (1) career, (2) family and relationships, (3) health and well-being, (4) hobbies and recreation, (5) finance, and (6) personal and spiritual development.

her office reminding all of her clients and herself of the special care, attention, and devotion she has to her clients and her profession.

Ideally, your business mission statement will define your target market, your products and services, and the benefits that you provide. Anthony Putman, in his book *Marketing Your Services,* recommends that a business mission statement include:

- What you sell
- Who you sell to
- Why your customers do business with you

If you work for a company, your statement might include:

- What you do that is of value and benefit

- Who benefits from what you do (within either the company or the client base)

- Why you are the best person to do what you do

Possible formats for your business or career mission statement are:

"My business mission is to support...in their desire to...by means of..."

"The purpose of my business is to provide...with...so that..."

"My career mission is to utilize my...(skills, expertise) to provide...so that..."

Here are some examples:

"My business mission is to support busy professionals in their desire to have their business trips be economical and hassle-free by providing a full range of travel services."

"My business mission is to use my financial knowledge and expertise to provide accurate financial information to the executives of XYZ Company so that they can make decisions that lead to success and profitability for the company."

"My career mission is to be the best in my field and to use my interior design skills to bring beauty, style, and elegance to the homes and offices of my clients in a way that enhances their lives."

"My career mission is to continually develop my leadership, negotiation, and marketing skills so that as a marketing executive I will be a leader in having the companies I work for open new international markets."

 **Create Your Business or Career Mission Statement**

Answer the following questions to help you develop your business or career mission statement:

What is the product, service, or skill that I offer?

What is the value and benefit of what I offer or do?

Who benefits from my product, service, or skill?

My business or career mission statement:

BELIEVE IN YOURSELF

Most people have very little awareness of how valuable they can be as a resource. You are a wealth of information, ideas, contacts, and resources. However, you must believe that this is true and train yourself to think and respond as someone who has value to offer. A positive sense of self, an awareness of the value you can be to others, and a positive attitude all contribute to your networking. If you downplay your strengths, have a low sense of self-esteem or confidence, and don't think you have anything to offer others, you will miss out on the opportunity to be a resource to others. Give some attention to developing a positive attitude about your networking ability.

Ways I Can Be of Value to Others:

☑ Introduce people to other people I know

☑ Recommend products and services that have benefited me

☑ Share information that I have learned through my success and failures

☑ Provide feedback regarding ideas

☑ Provide encouragement

☑ Share my expertise

☑ Brainstorm and contribute ideas

☑ Learn about other people's businesses and products so that I can promote and refer business to them

☑ Provide a new insight or idea

☑ Send others information I come across that could be of interest and value to them

Your ability to be clear and focused about your goals, purpose, and mission will enhance your networking effectiveness. Take good care of yourself. Respect your own power by being a valuable resource for others.

PAUSE Five Ways People Can Use You Best

List five things you could offer as a resource. Then list the people who could get value from what you have to offer.

REMINDERS

- *Awareness of your purpose, mission, and goals will keep you focused, on track, and effective with your networking.*

- *Where there is vision, people flourish.*

- *You are a wealth of information, ideas, contacts, and resources.*

91

CHAPTER TEN

THE POWER OF SMALL TALK

" Each person's life is lived as a series of conversations. "

—Deborah Tannen

J

JUST AS IT'S THE LITTLE THINGS that make a difference in building strong relationships, it's small talk that develops the rapport that leads to information, opportunities, and strong connections. People tend not to like the idea of small talk because there seems to be no purpose, no agenda; it seems frivolous. If you think that small talk is insignificant chitchat, think again. It is the gateway to business, referrals, job opportunities, and newfound friends.

In their book *Great Connections: Small Talk and Networking for Businesspeople,* Anne Baber and Lynne Waymon describe networking as "small talk with a purpose." It is a style of conversation. It is the first stage of conversation, an exploratory stage. During small talk people are paving the way for the conversation to grow into unknown territory. Small talk is the seed from which the conversation and the relationship grow.

I NEVER KNOW WHAT TO SAY!

One key to small talk is listening. Use what the other person is saying as the natural lead. So many people are thinking about how to say something smart, clever, or impressive that they miss their cues. The person who is talking is always giving cues about what to say or ask. Larry King, in his book *How to Talk to Anyone, Anytime, Anywhere,* says, "My first rule of conversation is this: I never learn a thing while I'm talking. . . . [So] if I'm going to learn I'll have to do it by listening. . . . Careful listening makes you better able to respond—to be a good talker when it's your turn. Good follow-up questions are the mark of a good conversationalist." He also recommends asking questions "that other persons will enjoy answering. Encourage them to talk about themselves and their accomplishments." The principles of small talk are the same whether you're at a small dinner party, a wedding, a conference, or a corporate meeting. King says, "Be open. Find the common ground with your partner. And, always, listen."

Networking takes place during conversation, and opportunities for conversations with people exist all around you— on airplanes, on elevators, in grocery store lines, at sporting events, conferences, and workshops. Wherever people are, conversation is possible, and anytime there's conversation, networking is possible. Conversation happens because someone takes the initiative to reach out, make contact, generate an interaction. The opportunities are endless. The problem is that most people have a comfort zone that gets in the way of making contact with other people.

Notice your comfort zone. Are you at ease making conversation with someone you don't know at a conference or convention? Do you avoid making eye contact with people in elevators and airplanes? Can you respond easily when someone tries to include you in a conversation? Learning to approach people with confidence is a professional skill that can serve anyone in any industry. It is not about making people talk or cornering people on elevators, but about your ability to open the door to conversation with the people right around you. As you develop this skill, you will notice that people are much more available than you had realized. Sometimes all it takes is a smile, a hello, or a simple comment.

THE LUCK FACTOR

Max Gunther, in his book *The Luck Factor,* defines the luckiest men and women as "those who have taken the trouble to form a great many friendly contacts with other people." People with a friendly manner tend to talk to others easily and this leads to friendships and opportunities. Gunther gives a telling example of two women, Catherine and Evelyn, who went to school together and worked together in an insurance company. Catherine's friendly nature prompted her to talk to "anybody who turned up near her." In the company cafeteria she commonly would engage in casual lunch-hour conversations with people she didn't know because the company was large and most employees were strangers to each other. One of her lunch-hour acquaintances passed her in the hall one day and, seeing her and remembering their conversation, he suddenly realized that she would be the perfect person to consider for a job opening in the personnel department. This seemed like a stroke of luck to Evelyn, who had never approached anyone in the cafeteria in a friendly or interested manner. Was it luck? It seemed like it even to Catherine, because the opportunity had come to her from " 'a man I hardly knew.' " Yet she had positioned herself to "receive that luck by making herself known to people."

Catherine's story had only just begun. She moved up within the insurance firm to assistant personnel director. Then one day she got a call from an executive recruiter who was prepared to pay generously to get the right person to hire as personnel director for a major bank. Catherine had all the right experience and qualities for the job. Luck again? It may seem that way until you find out how that executive recruiter found her. Catherine had recently attended a seminar on job rights where, in her usual manner, she initiated a conversation with one of the professors as they walked across campus.

The professor learned about Catherine's career path and was touched by her open, friendly enthusiasm. When he was contacted by the executive recruiter, he paused before responding, "'Wait a minute. It just happens I was talking with a woman here last week who. . . . Now, if I can only remember her name. . .'"

That professor was just one of hundreds of contacts Catherine habitually made each year. She had no thought or plan that the conversation would lead to the tremendous job opportunity it gave her. Evelyn never progressed with her career, while Catherine made significant strides. Her habit of befriending people "wasn't deliberately designed to bring her lucky breaks. She made contact with people for the sake of the contact itself. She simply found people enjoyable. Only in retrospect did she realize that this was the main channel through which some of her luckiest events had flowed."

AIRPLANE SMALL TALK

97

Marianne Smith, president of Creative Resource Seminars of Houston, says that during five years when she traveled extensively while working for an international high-tech company, she rarely talked to anyone on the airplane. Her routine was to bury herself in her work papers as soon as the plane took off and keep herself busy until the plane landed. She only got into small talk if someone else initiated it and she felt as if she had to respond. After reading about networking, she decided to try a new approach on a flight from Houston to Casper, Wyoming. She started a conversation with the man sitting next to her and found out that he was considering moving to Houston. They had a wonderful conversation during the entire flight. Marianne gave him a lot of information about Houston and passed along several referrals for his wife to follow up on regarding possible job opportunities in the medical industry. When they realized that they both had a layover in Denver, they decided to have lunch together and continue their networking. Marianne says that from then on she was hooked!

Her next experience, on a trip from Boston to Houston, reinforced her newfound enthusiasm. The person sitting next to her this time was a museum director who turned out to be a very pleasant, interesting, and entertaining person. When Marianne mentioned that she was going to Williamsburg, Virginia, the next week, he gave her the scoop on things to do and places to eat in Williamsburg (he was very familiar with the area because he had attended the College of William and Mary). One of the places he recommended was a restaurant she probably would have had no way of knowing about except through someone telling her. The restaurant was so good that she and her friends went there twice and declared that those were the two best meals of their entire trip!

▨ REACHING OUT TO PEOPLE

While I was signing books after a speaking engagement in Atlanta, one of the women who had been in my session came over to tell me how she had immediately put into practice what she had heard in my program. At the end of the program she turned to the woman sitting next to her and said, "In the spirit of what we have just heard, I would like to introduce myself. My name is Judy Vitucci." The other person graciously responded, saying who she was and what she did. It turned out that she worked for the company Judy had been trying to get an interview with for a job. When Judy told her this, the woman responded in a very positive and helpful manner with the name and phone number of the person Judy needed to meet. She went on to give her information about the contact and the company and offered her support. This woman was sitting right next to her! Judy could easily have walked away from that session without ever saying a word and she never would have known the opportunity she missed. You never know what resources are available right around you and what opportunities you may have walked by or walked away from. However, you can begin to benefit

Expand Your Comfort Zone

Answer the following questions to help you begin to expand your comfort zone.

What steps am I willing to take to expand my comfort zone?

In what settings am I willing to take the initiative to approach people?

Who do I know who is good at generating conversations with new people?

What do I notice about this person that can be helpful?

99

from some of what is available by reaching out to people in the spirit of networking.

David Burrows and his wife regularly attend ball games at their children's high school. At one of the games David struck up a conversation with the man sitting next to him. During the conversation, David mentioned that his daughter had recently graduated from college and was looking for work. The man encouraged David to have his daughter bring a copy of her résumé to the next ball game. She did and as a result she got a phone call from the man the following week that led to an interview and a job. She had been on her job search for seven months prior to that ball game.

MAKE THINGS HAPPEN

Take the initiative in approaching people, starting a conversation, introducing yourself, and offering your hand. The majority of the time, you'll find that people will respond in kind with a smile, introduction, and handshake. Larry King emphasizes, "Talk should not be a challenge, a grim obligation, or a way of filling up time. Talk is mankind's greatest invention, it's how we make connections among us, and it's one of the pleasures that life has to offer. Think of every conversation as an opportunity." "Whether you're sitting across a table from somebody or typing messages across a computer network," he says, "the principles of good talk are the same. It's all about making a connection with the other person. Openness, enthusiasm, and a willingness to listen will make you a popular conversationalist in any medium." The art of conversation builds rapport, develops relationships, and provides a basis for networking.

R E M I N D E R S

- *Networking happens through conversation.*
- *Being a conversation initiator opens the door to unexpected opportunities.*
- *People are often waiting for someone else to break the ice.*
- *Small talk leads to big results.*

100

CHAPTER ELEVEN

THE POWER OF LISTENING

" Listening is a magnetic and strange thing. The friends who listen to us are the ones we move toward, and we want to sit in their radius. "

—Karl Menninger

POOR LISTENING SKILLS CAN LEAD to misunderstandings, hurt feelings, and missed opportunities. Learning the power of listening will accelerate your ability to make immediate connections with people, develop trust and rapport quickly, and build strong relationships that lead to greater satisfaction and results.

Listening is the heart of communication. It is by listening to others that you learn. Many people are pretending to listen when they are actually waiting to talk or thinking about what they are going to say or do next. If you and I start talking at an association meeting and I focus on telling you all about my business's products and services and then I walk away, what have I gained? Nothing. I already knew everything I told you. If, instead, I put my focus on getting you to talk and learning about who you are, who you know, and what you are looking for, I walk away richer because I've added information to my network. It may or may not seem as though that information will be of immediate value to me, yet it may be useful to someone else in my network. Or it may be of value to me in the future. And, if I decide to follow up with you after our meeting, I can call you based on what I learned about you, not on what I think you need to know about me. Information is power and information is gained through listening—not "pretend" listening but real listening, where information is both heard and retained.

You know people who could benefit from meeting people you know, and you are the common link. Listen for opportunities to give to others. As you listen and learn more about your friends, clients, and business associates, you will discover more ways to be a resource for them. Pay attention when people talk about their personal interests, hobbies, and families. Make notes to yourself to recall these details so that you can send them newspaper clippings and magazine articles relating to their areas of interest.

Listen to your clients and when you hear them talking about something they need, step in and offer help. For example, "I want you to meet Jack Clark. He's working on a project similar to yours and I think it would be good for you two to meet. Suppose I set up a lunch to introduce you?" Or "Here is the name of someone I recommend that you call. He has one of the fastest-growing public relations firms in town and I think you would find it worthwhile to talk to him about the international media exposure that you want to generate for your firm." Listening and responding to your clients when there is nothing in it for you will help you to strengthen your relationships with them and reap rewards in the future.

Also listen to your customers to see what nonbusiness needs you can help fulfill. There are many opportunities to do this: recommending an auto mechanic, a florist, a dentist, a plumber, a travel agent, or an optometrist. If you are in sales, don't think you are done once you close the sale. The sale is just the beginning in building a client relationship that will lead to a lifetime of repeat business and referrals.

103

When you network with your clients or customers by giving them contacts and leads, you provide them with an additional benefit of doing business with you. By listening and responding to their needs, you are going the extra mile. You are adding value by thinking beyond what you can sell them and showing an interest in other aspects of their life and their business. This approach to being of service can set you apart from others in your industry. By being a good listener and resource, you can develop clients into lifetime customers.

FINE-TUNE YOUR ANTENNAS

Find out what people want and need. Listen for the following key phrases:

"I want . . ."

"I need . . ."

"I'm looking for . . ."

"I'm involved in a project that . . ."

"My goal is to . . ."

"I'm having a problem with . . ."

By listening, you'll find opportunities all around you to share information that can be helpful. Some time ago, I was speaking to the University of Houston Alumni Leadership Group. As people were arriving, I saw a woman I know and went over to say hello. While we were talking, a friend of hers came over and we were introduced. As she sat down, she mentioned how badly her back was hurting and said that she had been meaning to see someone about it all week. I responded by telling her that I have a friend who is a chiropractor, and I said that I would be glad to give her his name and number if she was interested. I pulled out my business card and wrote on the back: "Dr. Dana Harper, Chiropractor." I looked up his phone number in my daily planner, added the number to the information on the card, and handed it to her. She thanked me and stuck the card in her pocket, and I went on to conduct my program.

I never saw my friend's friend after that day. I didn't know if she would call Dr. Harper or not. But I knew I had done my part by offering the information. She had not requested the information, yet she had very clearly expressed a need. If she had said, "Oh, I already have a chiropractor. I just need to make an appointment," that would have been fine. She could easily have found someone to call by asking a friend or looking in the phone book. However, this way she had the information at her fingertips, and my job as a networker was done. It turns out that she did use the information. About a week later I received an envelope from Dr. Harper's office with a Harper Chiropractic T-shirt and a thank-you note for referring her. I was pleased. My friend, Dana Harper, has a new client and a new acquaintance has a pain-free back. Even though this may seem like a simple example, that one piece of information may have made the difference in helping her to handle a problem that had been bothering her for a whole week.

People sometimes hesitate to offer information or ideas to others. They may think, "It's none of my business" or "They didn't ask, so who am I to think they might want to know about this?" If you offer information with no strings attached and no expectations of reciprocation, I think you will find most people receptive and appreciative. Listening, sharing, and passing useful information along to others is a hallmark of the master networker.

Guidelines for Powerful Listening:

1. Show interest in people and what they are saying.

2. Make eye contact and focus on the other person.

3. Give your full attention to what is being said.

4. Be eager to learn something from the conversation.

5. Listen with the intent of gathering information, connecting, and developing rapport.

6. Listen for commonalities.

7. Listen for information that can open the door
   to networking.

Networking conversations are not the place to teach, preach, impress, or one-up. Make your conversations interesting, engaging, and informative. And remember, a monologue is not a conversation. A conversation is a flow between people that involves knowing when to respond, when to listen, when to ask, and when to offer.

Respond to What You Hear:

The following phrases can be used to respond to the needs of others:

> *"Based on what you just said about needing..., I know someone who would be a good person for you to talk to."*

> *"If I could schedule a lunch meeting with you and ..., would that be helpful?"*

> *"I heard you were looking for... XYZ Company is hiring. The person to call is..."*

> *"I just thought of someone you might enjoy talking to because..."*

> *"It sounds as if what would be helpful is... Here's the name and number of the person I used when I was dealing with this same issue last month."*

> *"This may or may not be exactly what you're looking for, but Jack Doe has a business that..."*

> *"I don't know if they're hiring, but here's the name of someone at ABC Company."*

LISTENING CREATES CONNECTION AND NOURISHMENT

People tend to think that they need to talk to be noticed and remembered. However, listening can be the key to having people remember you. When you really listen, which means giving fully of yourself to someone at that moment, a connection happens that will cause that person to remember you in a special way for a long time. The act of listening touches people at a level where they can connect and therefore remember you. Listening kindles our connections and strengthens our relationships.

Listening is instrumental in connecting with people in a way that builds trust, rapport, and relationship. People in our society are hungry to be heard. Everyone's talking and yet few people feel really heard and understood. Michael Nichols, in *The Lost Art of Listening,* says, "To listen well we must forget ourselves and submit to the other person's need for attention." If everyone is trying to get attention, then possibly no one is actually getting the attention that he or she hopes for.

Make sure that you have people in your life and your network with whom you have a good listening relationship. If your attention needs are met, you will be better able to listen and give attention to others without getting anxious about having your turn. As Nichols says, "Regardless of how much we take it for granted, the importance of listening cannot be overestimated. The gift of our attention and understanding makes other people feel validated and valued. Our ability to listen, and listen well, creates goodwill that comes back to us. But effective listening is also the best way to enjoy others, to learn from them, and to make them interesting to be with."

You can usually tell when someone is not really listening to you. Typically you can even sense over the phone when someone is just barely paying attention to your conversation. Not listening harms a relationship because it leaves people feeling discounted and overlooked. However, true listening will enhance a relationship tremendously as it generates a feeling of connection, interest, and value. Rapport is developed not just by what you say but by the cadence of your interchange, the rhythm of listening and talking that flows easily between two people when they both feel included, respected, and appreciated.

Unfortunately, many people think they are better at listening than they really are. The problem is that they tend to take listening for granted and think that as long as they are not talking or interrupting, they are listening. But listening is not the same as not talking. "To listen well, it's necessary to let go of what's on your mind long enough to hear what's on the other person's," Michael Nichols tells us. "Feigned attentiveness doesn't work." Listening involves paying attention, showing an interest, and validating the speaker. "Human beings require nourishment to grow up strong but also to maintain their strength and vitality," he says. "Listening nourishes our sense of worth. All of us . . . need attention to sustain us."

One of the benefits of my involvement in The Windsor Club is participating with my Roundtable Group. Seven of us meet once a month and serve as an advisory board for each other. One of the most valuable aspects of these meetings is that we have an attentive group of peers who give attention while encouraging us to talk about our business. This process of talking to people who are your friends and peers typically leads to greater clarity, renewed enthusiasm, and fresh ideas. It is understandable to get discouraged or frustrated sometimes. Yet often when we try to talk about our difficulties, people respond by trying to cheer us up, by pointing out all the reasons we shouldn't feel that way, or by giving pointed advice. Sometimes the greatest gift we can give others is nonjudgmental, supportive listening that honors their thinking and allows them to release their thoughts and move on to new ideas and horizons.

"When we're with someone who's interested and responsive— a good listener—we perk up and come alive. When we're with someone who doesn't listen, we shut down," Michael Nichols reminds us. "Being listened to is as vital to our enthusiasm for life as love and work." Make sure that you have people in your life who give you that nourishment by listening with all of their being. And make sure that you develop your ability to listen and be a source of nourishment for the people in your network.

Be a Better Listener

To develop your power of listening, answer these questions:

In what types of situations do I tend to not listen well?

In which relationships do I know I want to be a better listener?

What will I do to become a better listener?

R E M I N D E R S

- *Listening nourishes, validates, and energizes.*
- *Through listening we access information that broadens our network.*
- *Listening is the heart of communication.*
- *Listening creates a strong, long-lasting, positive connection.*

THE POWER
OF SPEAKING UP

*"The whole art of life is knowing the
right time to say things."*

—Maeve Binchy, Irish writer

ARE YOU ONE OF THOSE PEOPLE who grew up hearing the phrase "Don't toot your own horn!" and you've responded by going to the other extreme? If so, it's time you learned to *speak up!* Speaking up is not about tooting your own horn; it is about not hiding your light under a bushel! You don't have to brag or be aggressive to speak up. You can present yourself in a way that honors your own personality and style while at the same time conveying pride and confidence. Your ability to speak in a positive and professional manner about who you are and what you do helps you to find the clients, friends, and job opportunities you are looking for.

You convey an impression of yourself with everything you say and do. The first few minutes of a job interview set the tone for the interview. The first five minutes of a sales presentation make a difference in gaining the attention and interest of your prospect. When you introduce yourself to a group of people, you have only a few seconds to get their attention in a way that makes a positive, lasting impression.

THE PERFECT INTRODUCTION

When you introduce yourself, you have the perfect opportunity to convey who you are and what you do so people can connect with you and know how to network with you. Your introduction is the opportunity to develop that first stepping-stone of a relationship. Most people miss this opportunity because they introduce themselves by merely giving their name, their title, and the name of their company. There's nothing wrong with this type of introduction, but it does not typically generate relationship and rapport because it only gives people data. Instead, include in your introduction a phrase or tag line that helps people to relate to and remember you.

Whether you are introducing yourself to a roomful of people or someone you just met, make sure that you connect and that the other people walk away with a positive experience. This will reinforce the likelihood that they will remember who you are and what you do.

Sample Introductions:

> *"Hello, I'm Mark Hargrove, Hargrove Design Group. I enjoy doing what I've been doing since I was three— drawing, coloring, and creating beauty on paper."*

> *"My name is Greg Richardson. I work with business-people to protect their business ideas, products, and materials. I am a patent and copyright attorney with William, Blanchard & Jackson."*

> *"Good morning. My name is Linda Doodeheefver, owner of Salon Entre Nous. We pamper you from head to toe so that you look and feel your best."*

113

"Good morning. I'm George Scott. My wife and I own Best Business Forms. We give you quality printed products, everything from business forms to specialty items to annual reports."

"Hello. My name is Dana Harper. I am a chiropractor and I help people lead lives free of pain and discomfort."

"Good morning. I'm Marilyn Jones, your friendly local dentist. I'm gentle and compassionate while I restyle your smile."

"Hello. My name is Jan Tyler. My greatest accomplishment in life has been teaching young people to learn job skills. I'm a teacher at Independence High School."

Here are some key phrases suitable for introductions:

"I love helping people . . ."

"I make sure my clients . . ."

"I enjoy . . ."

"I am committed to working with people to . . ."

"I am dedicated to . . ."

"I love working with . . . to . . ."

"My focus is to . . ."

Keep your introduction clear, concise, and personable so that it flows easily and naturally. Speak about the value and benefit of who you are and what you offer.

In your introduction, it is standard to say the greeting and name first, followed by the company information and key phrase. However, in certain industries it is sometimes good to say your key phrase and then give the company information, so that you make the personal connection first. Some people, after they hear words such as *attorney, CPA, financial planner,* or *insurance agent,* will immediately "check out." Either they think they already know what the other person does and therefore don't need to listen or they have a certain notion of the industry that influences the way they listen to the rest of the introduction. If you're not sure what order works best for your introduction, say it out loud several different ways and see what sounds best. You can also try it both ways with other people to find out what works best to generate the kind of response you want.

Also, make sure you speak so that others understand. Cheryl Watson, associate professor at The University of Texas Medical Branch in Galveston, noticed a major difference in the way people responded to her depending on how she introduced herself. When she used her industry's terminology and introduced herself as a "molecular endocrinologist," people didn't know how to respond. Using a simpler statement, "I study how hormones work. I'm a professor at the University of Texas," she never fails to generate an interesting conversation.

During a job search, Steve Hammett realized that most people did not understand what he meant when he would introduce himself as a reservoir engineer. He came up with "I coax the oil out of the ground. I'm a reservoir engineer." He has noticed that people respond more positively to this simple, nontechnical introduction, which makes them feel as if they can talk with him in common, everyday language and still learn more about what he does. It is very important to use words and terms that anyone can understand (pretend that you are telling a young person what you do).

John Hall found that his title, administrative director of educational/student support services, was nebulous, cumbersome, difficult to say, and difficult to understand. He receives much more positive attention and interest when he introduces himself with a simpler approach: "I work with children and their families to help kids stay in school and be employable when they graduate."

Jack Horn used to feel uncomfortable saying that he was the president of his company because he thought it would sound too forbidding and people might then hesitate to approach him. So he started off his introduction by saying, "My name is Jack Horn, with Universal Financial Services . . ." However, when he switched his introduction to say, "My name is Jack Horn, president of Universal Financial Services . . . ," he

115

found the opposite to be true. More people approached him because they knew he was the one with the knowledge and authority to take care of their needs and interests.

You might create an introduction that is catchy, humorous, or a play on words; this is fine if it fits your own style and personality. However, if you are in a serious industry and you try to be cute and funny, it may backfire. If your words are catchy and upbeat but you have a frown on your face, again, people will receive mixed signals. If you are in what is supposed to be a friendly, service-oriented business and you come across as stiff and cold, people may feel a bit confused and not know why. Think about your personality, your industry, how you come across, what you want to convey, what you want people to remember about you. Your introduction will either turn people off, leave them cold, or draw them in. It's up to you. And remember, it's not only the words that communicate. Your tone of voice, smile, eye contact, enthusiasm, and body language all convey a message, so make sure that your words and your body language are congruent with the image you wish to project.

When I'm working with a group where everyone is in the same industry or with the same company, the introductions are still different because each person is unique. Think about it: no matter what you do, there must be many other people out there doing the same thing. What's going to make you stand out? What's going to cause people to remember you? There is always something unique about you, what you offer, the way you conduct your business, the level of service you provide, or the special expertise you have developed. This uniqueness can be presented in a very simple manner in your introduction, so that you create positive, lasting visibility for yourself.

"WHAT DO YOU DO?"

Most of the examples up to now have been of introductions that would be used in front of a group. However, very often you must introduce yourself to one person. You can take the

Develop a Powerful Self-Introduction

Answer the following questions to develop an effective introduction:

What do I love most about what I do?

What do I want people to know about me?

What do I want people to think of when they think of my business?

What is the beneficial difference that my product or service makes in the lives of my clients?

What is the emotional benefit of my service or product for people?

What problem does my product or service solve?

What is the value of what I offer?

What do I want to be known for?

What is special or unique about my product, my service, or the way I do business?

What is my ideal market?

What words can I use that represent me and help to generate rapport with people?

My introduction:

117

same introduction that you would use in front of a group and simplify it to respond to the individual who asks, "What do you do?" or "What type of business are you in?" When people ask you what you do, rather than responding with a title, describe what you can do for them. Your focus should always be on speaking about what you can do for people:

> *"What do you do?" / "I help people find their dream home."*

> *"Where do you work?" / "At the university. I organize career placement services for our students."*

> *"What kind of business are you in?" / "Property management. We manage and maintain office space for our clients."*

How you present and position yourself can change the way people respond to you, turning strangers into prospects and prospects into clients.

PRACTICE MAKES PERFECT

You know how easy it is to say your name. That's because you have done so millions of times throughout your life. The same thing can happen with your introduction. Practice saying it out loud while driving in the car by yourself. Practice saying it to yourself in front of a mirror. Practice it with different facial expressions, various inflections, various personas. Through practice, your introduction can become as simple, easy, and natural as saying your name.

Benefits of a Powerful Presentation:

- ☑ You connect with people.
- ☑ People relate and therefore respond to you.
- ☑ You are remembered in a positive manner.
- ☑ You are seen as approachable.

☑ It saves time.

☑ It generates more business potential.

☑ You develop greater confidence.

☑ You present a professional image.

☑ It provides an opportunity to convey value and benefit.

☑ It generates a sense of relationship.

Your appearance, your words, and your tone of voice all convey a message to the people around you. If you are not getting the response you want from others, think about what you would like to change about the message you are sending. Let people know what you love to do and how you can serve them. Business is about serving people, and one of the ways you serve people is by letting them know who you are and what you have to offer, so that if they want and need what you have they can easily find you.

119

R E M I N D E R S

■ *Speaking with pride and confidence is not about tooting your own horn; it is about not hiding your light under a bushel. Let your light shine!*

■ *Always speak about the value and benefit of who you are and what you do.*

■ *Learn to speak about what you do in a positive, professional manner so that the people who want and need what you have can find you.*

CHAPTER THIRTEEN

THE POWER
OF ASKING

*"**A**sking for help does not mean that we are weak or incompetent. It usually indicates an advanced level of honesty and intelligence."*

—Anne Wilson Schaef

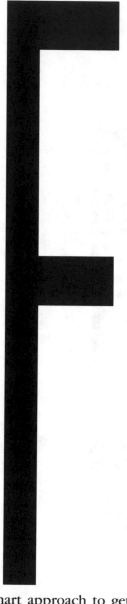

FOR OVER FIVE YEARS I've been asking my audiences how they feel when someone calls to sincerely ask them for help. The usual response is: "I feel flattered, honored, great, acknowledged, glad to help!" People want to contribute, but you have to be the one to reach out, to let others know what you need, and to give them permission to get involved. The first step in developing the power of asking is to shift your attitude about asking for help. Asking for help, support, and information is a smart approach to getting things done.

Asking is a very important part of networking. Yet commonly, when people get to the point of even thinking of asking for assistance, they fall back into the independence mentality discussed in Chapter Five. Thoughts that tend to get in the way of asking include "I don't want to bother him,"

"She's too busy," and "I should be able to figure this out myself." Asking is critical because it is up to you to let people know what you need, what you want, and what you are looking for.

How to Be Effective with Your Requests:

☑ Be clear about what you want.

☑ Ask for what you want.

☑ Make your request as concise and specific as possible.

☑ Make your request with no demands and no strings attached.

☑ Ask in such a way that people feel acknowledged and included.

☑ Ask often.

If you have trouble asking for help, it may be because you don't like to turn people down. Do you feel comfortable saying no to others? Do you sometimes say yes and then feel trapped when you realize that you really wanted to say no? If this is the case, then your first step is to learn to say no when it is the appropriate response. I noticed that as I gained in my own strength and sense of self and began to discern when to say no and stick to it, it actually became easier for me to ask others. So now I ask more often, and even though I may get more noes, I get a lot more yesses than ever.

My commitment is to do the best that I can for my network. Sometimes people make requests I can't respond to because I don't have the information, contacts, or ideas they are looking for. I still do the best I can to point them in the right direction. And I trust the people in my network to do their best for me.

YOU NEVER KNOW UNTIL YOU ASK

Lilly Aranda works as secretary to the president of Houston Community College. As a participant in a program called Project Future Perfect, which was designed to teach diversity and leadership skills, she was asked to get a mentor. The two people she thought of, Houston police chief Sam Nuchia and Mary Keegan, founder and executive director of the End Hunger Network, are very busy people and she was skeptical that they would even consider such a request. She decided to contact them anyway.

She sent letters to both. Two years earlier, Lilly had attended a luncheon where Mary Keegan was the speaker and she got to meet her. One of the things Lilly remembered about that luncheon program was Mary's encouragement to never give up and never take no for an answer. Two years later she followed through on that advice by asking Mary to be her mentor! Lilly heard back from Mary Keegan in one week and had the opportunity to watch her in action while attending various board meetings with her.

Later, Lilly also received a letter back from the police chief and thus ended up with two very powerful leadership mentors. She learned that he had never before been asked to be a mentor and was very honored by her request. It would have been easy in both of these situations to judge that these people would be too busy or shouldn't be bothered, or to feel unworthy of asking. Hats off to Lilly for asking and seizing the opportunity to work alongside two leaders she truly admired.

Sample Networking Requests:

> *"Who do you know with experience in getting on the Internet?"*
>
> *"I'm looking for a veterinarian. Who do you recommend?"*
>
> *"I am in the midst of a project at work and I need support with making long-range projections. Who do you recommend I talk to?"*
>
> *"Who should I know given that I am new in town and want to find out about networking events?"*
>
> *"Who do you recommend I talk to about my upcoming trip to Australia?"*
>
> *"What do you recommend I do to take my product line international?"*

"Who do you think it would be best for me to talk to about a position within your company?"

TELEPHONE PROTOCOL

A great deal of networking happens over the phone, through answering machines, voice mail, E-mail, and fax machines. Leslie Smith, associate director of the National Association of Female Executives, emphasizes the importance of avoiding "telephone networking blunders." "Unfortunately," she says, "the anonymity of the telephone sometimes causes networkers to be lax about protocol." However, as with any type of networking, she notes, "It is not what you ask for but how you ask for it."

Here are some tips for making the most of telephone contacts.

Do Your Homework

Gather information about the contact by asking questions of the person giving you the contact. Find out what you and the contact have in common.

125

Prepare for the Call

Take a minute to ask yourself these questions:

Why are you calling this person?

What do you want from the call?

Where did you meet the person you're calling?

Who referred you to the person you're calling?

What do you want to learn and/or ask for?

What do you want to have happen as a result of the call?

How can you ask for another contact?

What can you offer this person?

Evaluate the questions you want to ask to see if they are the best questions to ask of this person. Make sure the questions are specific enough to make it easy for the other person to respond. Finally, get yourself into a positive frame of mind for making the call.

Make the Call

Once a member of your network has recommended that you call someone, make the call as promptly as possible. It is great to be able to say:

> *"I just got off the phone with... They recommended that I give you a call."*

> *"I had breakfast with... this morning and she gave me your name and number."*

> *"I met you recently at the... conference in Atlanta. I wanted to follow up on our conversation about..."*

Be direct and immediately let the person know who you are, why you are calling, and how you got his or her name and number. Ask for permission. Say, "Is this a good time to talk?" or "Do you have a few minutes to talk?" If the other person indicates that it is not a good time, ask when you should call back. Then make a note to yourself so that you can call back at the time requested. Summarize the call, thank the other person, and offer your support. Ask, "What can I do for you?" or "How could I be of support to you?" or "What do you need that I might help with?" or "Thank you. If I can ever be of assistance, please let me know!"

When you are leaving messages on voice mail or an answering machine, make sure you speak clearly. Give your name and phone number twice to make it easy for the other person to verify it while writing it down. You may also want to indicate when the best time is to reach you.

Approach Each Contact with an Open Mind

Don't compare or prejudge, and let go of preconceived notions. Every call can lead to another contact, the informa-

Identify What You Want

Answer the following questions to identify what you want to request of your network:

What short-term goals do I have for my business?

What long-term goals do I have for my business?

What goals do I have for other areas of my life?

What information or contact would help me get where I want?

What requests can I make of my network to help me accomplish each of my most recent or most important goals?

Which people in my network can I call on for each of these requests?

127

tion you are looking for, the appointment, the job, the sale, or an introduction to a new networking buddy. Develop your ability to ask questions and engage in conversation in order to generate the rapport and the information that you are looking for. If you find out that the person you have called is not really the best person for you to talk to, you can always ask who she or he recommends that you contact next.

▇ POST-CALL ACTIVITY

Make note of any of the following actions that are to take place as a result of your call:

☑ Follow up in six months.

☑ Send a thank-you note for the information.

☑ Send a packet and then follow up in five days.

☑ Send reference letters.

☑ Send a résumé.

☑ Send a brochure.

☑ Send testimonial letters.

☑ Send information that would be of value to the other person.

☑ Call back with the number of someone you want to refer to the other person.

☑ Notify the person who gave you the information or referral that you followed through.

I'M CALLING YOU BECAUSE . . .

You call people for a particular reason. Let them know why you thought of them and what is special about them that caused you to ask for their assistance. This acknowledges them, helps to establish immediate rapport, and primes the pump for them to begin to think about how they can respond.

> *"I've heard very good things about XYZ Company and I know you've worked there for several years. I want to know who you would recommend I talk to about possible opportunities there."*

> *"You have been so successful at . . . that I wanted to ask you about . . ."*

> *"I'm planning on moving to Washington and I know you have a lot of good contacts there through your years of . . ."*

> *"You know so many people, I thought you would be the best person to ask about . . ."*

128

I AM WRITING YOU BECAUSE...

You can also make requests in writing. In some of my training sessions, participants write a "letter of request." The purpose of this letter is to let others know how they can assist you in reaching a goal that is important to you.

Include the following elements in your letters to others:

1. Acknowledge them for what they mean to you or what they have done for you.

2. Tell them what your goal is and what this project means for you and your business.

3. Be specific regarding what they can do to help you accomplish your goal.

4. Give them an easy way to respond.

5. Let them know you are available to support them with their goals.

Items to Consider:

Do I want letters to go to: only a select few? all of my clients? everyone in my networking club? everyone on my data base?

What type of follow-up would be most effective?

Should I include a response form? a return envelope?

Do I address the letters by hand, print labels, or run the envelopes through the printer?

If you are sending a letter to a select group of people, you might customize it for each person and address and stamp the envelopes by hand. If you have a large list with a more general request for support, it may be more appropriate to do a mail merge, include a response form, and print the envelopes on the computer. You get to choose your approach based on

129

Sample Letter of Request

Dear _____ :

More than five years ago, I made a career decision to take Discovery Seminars from a part-time venture to a full-fledged, growing business. Through faith, persistence, and the power of networking, this business has grown in wonderful and miraculous ways! Thank you for being part of the support system that has made this possible. Knowing that I have people like you in my network gives me the strength and courage to move forward with my dreams and goals.

Over the past year I have been fortunate to expand my business, speaking at national and regional conventions and leading trainings for corporations from Vancouver to Memphis to Atlanta. I am writing to ask for your support in reaching additional contacts for these types of programs.

I would appreciate it if you would take five minutes of your time to write down the names of three people in companies or associations that I could contact about my trainings and keynote presentations.

For your convenience I have enclosed a response form and a self-addressed, stamped envelope. I look forward to hearing from you. Please, also, let me know what I can do for you.

Fond regards,

 **Worksheet for Your Letter of Request**

Answer the following questions. Then write your letter!

What is the goal or project for which I want support?

What will it mean to me to accomplish my goal?

To whom should I send this letter?

What am I acknowledging this person for?

What can this person specifically do to help me accomplish my goal?

How do I want the person to respond?

What kind of support can I offer to this person?

131

who will get the letter and the image you want to convey. The main thing is to send the letter and invite people to respond.

When people ask you, "What do you need? How can I help? What can I do for you?" don't give the typical automatic response: "Oh, nothing, I'm fine." When people show an interest and willingness to be of service, give them some way to network with you. If you are always giving to others without allowing them to give and contribute to you, you are actually limiting those networking relationships. It is important for there to be a balance in the give-and-take in relationships.

Get in the habit of asking. Asking for support and information nurtures your network and gets that networking flow going.

R E M I N D E R S

- *People want to contribute, but you have to be the one to open the door and give them permission.*

- *Most people don't get what they're asking for because of the way they ask!*

- *Be specific and gracious with your requests.*

- *Even if someone you call can't help with what you are looking for, you have strengthened your relationship with that person by asking.*

132

CHAPTER FOURTEEN

THE POWER OF THINKING BIG

"Unless you choose to do great things with it, it makes no difference how much you are rewarded, or how much power you have."

—Oprah Winfrey

PEOPLE POWER

WHEN YOU NOTICE YOURSELF thinking, "I've called everyone I know," think again. The people you know are stepping-stones to the people they know and the list never ends. Your network is truly vast and unlimited. Think about all the people you grew up with, went to school with, worked with, met through friends and church meetings, and so on. It is estimated that people have anywhere from 250 to three thousand contacts. It is important to develop an awareness of the magnitude and reach of your network.

You never know until you take the time to get to know people what they may have to offer. So don't prejudge them, thinking, "Oh, they probably don't have any information about . . ." or "He probably doesn't know anyone who . . ." Remember that each and every person is a wealth of information, ideas, and contacts with connections to 250 additional people.

134

It's easy to get into the routine of talking with the same people all the time. Remember to keep an open and expanded outlook and reach into your network. Keep yourself from getting into a rut by staying aware of the people around you. Stay aware of your dreams and goals, stay aware of the vast universe that is available, and stay aware of the big picture of life while addressing the day-to-day issues that demand your attention.

PLANNING FOR THE FUTURE

I had the opportunity to speak in Dallas at the Mary Kay Cosmetics Annual Seminar several years ago. I conducted a program called "Networking for Business Growth" for the consultants and one called "Networking for Unit Growth" for the directors. It was obvious that many of these Mary Kay representatives were doing very well financially with their business and the newer consultants had the goal of following in their footsteps. In my program, I said, "I know you have big dreams. And I know with your energy, focus, and enthusiasm you can get there. I encourage you to focus on building a network now with the kind of people you are going to be calling on in the future. Don't wait until you need the financial planner; go out and find one now. Start looking for the person you can develop a relationship with so that when you're there, making that money, you'll already have someone in your network you have a relationship with and can trust, who knows you well enough to understand how to work with you and support you with your financial goals."

The same idea applies to you in all areas of your life. Who else will you need in your network once you reach a certain goal? Are they in your network now? If not, how can you start meeting them now so they will be in place before the need arises?

Maybe one of your goals is to travel around the world. Do you have a travel agent who can help you plan any kind of trip you want and who responds promptly to your needs? Do you enjoy working with that person? Find a travel agent

135

now so that you can build a good relationship and trust that person with all your business and personal travel plans.

How would you build your network if your goal were to buy a bed-and-breakfast inn in the mountains? What types of resources would be helpful in finding and buying an inn? Possibly a business broker, a banker, a CPA, and an attorney. Once you have bought the inn you might need an interior designer, a graphics designer for a brochure and announcements, maybe a remodeler for repairs and renovation, and a publicist to get the word out to the travel agents.

There are millions of people around who could be valuable resources in your life now and in the future. It is very smart to begin to consciously build your network so that the resources are in your network before you actually need them.

Building a network is like having a full dance card. Your "networking dance card" lists all the products and services you could possibly need or want in all areas of your life. By filling in the names of the people you already have in your support system, it becomes obvious where the gaps are and who you need to bring into your network.

A NETWORK THAT KEEPS ON GROWING

Several years ago, after focusing most of my energy on building my business in Houston, I decided to concentrate on expanding my business into other cities. I began to think about some of the areas where I wanted to do business and on my list was Colorado. I thought of a woman in Denver, Carol Ann Dovi, who had called after reading *Power Networking* to say how much she liked the book. We hit it off over the phone and stayed in touch. I called Carol one day and said, "I want to do some work in your area. You seem to be very well connected and know a lot of people. What do you think? Would you be willing to help set up some programs and speaking engagements? I want to come to town for a week, conduct some programs, meet some people, and generate other possibilities for the future." She said yes and we were on our way.

We picked a week and I began to schedule speaking engagements. I started announcing to the groups I was speaking to, "I'm going to be in Colorado on a speaking tour. Who do you suggest I contact?" I started gathering names and contacts, which led to speaking engagements. I also asked some of my Houston clients to refer me to their counterparts in Colorado. Carol called her contacts and between the two of us we scheduled eight programs for my one-week trip. It turned out to be a busy, wonderful, whirlwind trip.

YOU DON'T HAVE TO START OVER

When you have lived in one place for a long time and decide to move to a new city, it can feel as if you're starting over. Cindy and Alan Goldsberry had lived in Houston for thirteen years when they decided to move their family and their business to Atlanta. Because they planned well and made good use of their network, they were able to become established and known in their new city very quickly. Before they ever left Houston, they gathered the names of forty people in Atlanta from their Houston friends and associates. When they arrived in Atlanta, they got busy on the phone. For example, Ralph Hayes, president of Data Voice Technology in Houston, had given Alan the name and phone number of Harold Kolbe, who has the same kind of voice mail company in Atlanta that Ralph has in Houston. Alan called and said, "Hi, my name is Alan Goldsberry. I just moved here from Houston and Ralph Hayes recommended that I contact you about your voice mail service."

You don't have to start over when you are moving to a new city or expanding your business into a new geographic area. The best way to expand your network is through the people you already know; ask people in your current network to be stepping-stones to new contacts, new areas, and new possibilities.

137

Fill Your Networking Dance Card

Begin to purposefully and consciously build your network. Your dance card will be unique to you because it relates to your needs, interests, profession, life-style, and goals. Be sure to think about your current and long-term goals while you're developing your card.

List the products and services you use in all areas of your life. In the business and finance areas, you might include a CPA, a banker, an attorney, a graphics designer, a printer, a public relations firm, and a voice mail service.

In the area of health and well-being, you might include a doctor, a nutritionist, a massage therapist, a dentist, a counselor, and an optometrist.

For hobbies and recreation, you might list tennis partners, a golf pro, an art instructor, a yoga teacher, a personal fitness trainer, and a fishing guide, among others.

For your home, you might include a plumber, an air conditioning and heating service, a yard maintenance firm, a remodeling contractor, an electrician, and a pest control service.

In the personal area, you might include a manicurist, a hairdresser, a personal shopper, a florist, an auto repair shop, an alterations shop, a dry cleaners, and a jeweler.

Once you have listed all the categories you can think of, identify the people from your network who fit each category. The gaps show you who you need to add to your dance card to have a full network.

PASS IT ON

Networking is a form of recycling: instead of using things up and throwing them away, take the value that is there for you and then pass it on to others.

Think about all the information that comes across your desk. Do you take a moment to ask yourself: Who else would be interested in this information? When you hear about a valuable workshop or opportunity, do you ask yourself: Who could I fax or mail this information to? When you get good service from a business, do you ask yourself: Who would benefit from knowing about this company?

Networking is collecting and distributing information— not collecting to hoard it for yourself, but collecting to build a reservoir of information, contacts, and resources to draw on at any time for your own benefit and the benefit of the people in your network. Keep the networking flow going. Train yourself to listen and pass information on to others.

Think of yourself as a powerful resource who can easily contribute to the lives of others by being aware of every opportunity to pass it on!

139

A NETWORK WITH UNLIMITED REACH

One of the values of having a strong, full network is having easier access to people you want to reach. It is said that anyone you would want to meet or contact is only four to five people away from you. It may take a few phone calls to find the person you know who can provide a connection to the person you want to reach, and it may take some courage to reach out to people you don't know in this way. Yet this is what a support system is for: to provide links and support for you.

AUSE Stretch Your Reach

Who are some of the people you have never contacted because you thought they were out of your reach? List their names; then ask yourself the following questions about each one:

Why do I want to contact this person?

What do I think this person can do for me?

What could I do for this person?

Which of the people I know could be the link or stepping-stone in contacting this person?

R E M I N D E R S

- *You are only a few people away from anyone you would want to meet or contact.*

- *Every person you know or meet can be the connecting link to another 250 people.*

- *Don't prejudge people, because you never know what you might have in common or how you might be of support to one another!*

THE POWER OF COMMITMENT

> **"You** *are as powerful and strong*
> *as you allow yourself to be, and . . .*
> *the most difficult part of any endeavor is taking*
> *the first step, making the first decision.* **"**
>
> —Robyn Davidson

GOOD NETWORKING IDEAS ARE USELESS unless you supply energy, commitment, and action so that they become a new, integrated way of expressing yourself and relating to others. Action and commitment turn good ideas into positive, influential habits. The ideas in this book are not meant to be just "good ideas," but powerful tools for building, strengthening, and working with your support system.

The difference between a mediocre networker who occasionally produces results and experiences sporadic satisfaction and gratification and a master networker is the level of commitment they have, based on a deep awareness of the long-term value of networking. People in our society tend to be oriented toward immediate gratification. The greatest value of a support system is the long-term results and satisfaction generated by a lifetime network.

AUSE Strengthen Your Commitment

Answer the following questions to clarify and strengthen your commitment:

What am I currently most committed to in my life?

Which of the power principles discussed in the book will I implement in my life?

My new commitment to my support system is:

My new commitment to my networking approach is:

143

Making a commitment to your network means making a commitment to your life, and to having a life of richness that comes from full, nurturing, caring relationships and from pursuing your dreams and goals.

Stephen Covey says, "Without involvement, there is no commitment." He explains that you have two ways to put yourself in control of your life immediately: "Make a promise and keep it or set a goal and work to achieve it." By following through on your commitments and honoring them, you are establishing in yourself the honor, courage, and strength that help you to take on even more responsibility. Covey adds, "By making and keeping promises to ourselves and others, little by little, our honor becomes greater than our moods." It is easy to get distracted from your commitments and your goals. It is easy to let things slide and lose touch with people. The power of your commitment lies in the strength that comes from doing what you say, making something happen, and living in a way that is true to your beliefs. The power of honoring your commitments will allow you to develop the habits and life-style that give you what you want and desire in life.

Keeping a promise or commitment with someone is key in developing the trust and respect that build a powerful networking relationship. As Covey says, "If we can't make and keep commitments to ourselves as well as to others, our commitments become meaningless." A foundation of trust is built through honoring yourself and others to the best of your ability.

Knowing the power and importance of networking and *living* it are two different things. Until our understanding, wisdom, and desire are integrated into the very core of our existence, there is no power. The power of networking is in people and the way they show their care, trust, and interest in one another. It is human nature to care, and yet sometimes we forget to express that caring. Commitment provides the power to "remember" to live in a way that is true to the values and qualities that are important in life. Making a commitment to yourself, your relationships, and your values is the most powerful step you can take toward a life of richness.

144

R E M I N D E R S

- *Making a commitment to networking is making a commitment to your life.*

- *Commitment turns good ideas into powerful habits.*

- *Commitment develops honor and trust within yourself and with others.*

**STRENGTHENING
YOUR NETWORKING
POWER**

CHAPTER SIXTEEN

WHAT'S YOUR PEOPLE POWER PROFILE?

*"*To achieve you need thought.... You have to
know what you are doing and that's real power.*"*

—Ayn Rand

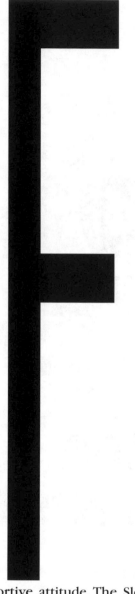

FIVE BASIC NETWORKING PROFILES are displayed on the People Power Profile Diagram: Zombie, Robot, Slouch, Dabbler, and Master. Each profile represents a different level of networking awareness, attitudes, habits, skills, and commitment. The Zombie lacks the awareness, attitudes, and habits for effective networking. The Robot has well-developed habits but is underdeveloped in terms of a powerful, supportive attitude. The Slouch has a well-developed, positive attitude but lacks the power of having strong habits. The Dabbler is somewhat developed in both areas but lacks the commitment and practice that constitute mastery. And, of course, the Master has developed the ultimate in both attitude and habits.

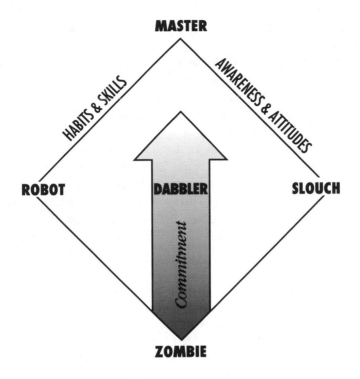

People Power Profile Diagram

THE ZOMBIE

Zombies are unaware. It's not that they can't network successfully. It's not that they don't have the ability. They just don't have the required information or awareness. The Zombie is "asleep" to the possibilities and opportunities that networking holds out.

Zombies don't even realize that there are professional associations, trade conventions, skill-building seminars and conferences, and networking clubs for them to join and attend. If they hear about a convention, it is usually because someone tells them about it at the last moment. They arrive with no business cards and walk around observing what is going on but not really knowing how to participate and get involved. It doesn't occur to Zombies to approach people at the convention and generate conversation, or to initiate a follow-up afterward.

Zombies typically think that their job is secure and that the company will always take care of them. They don't understand that they need to be actively in charge of their own career. Rather than managing their career, they expect it to progress of its own accord.

In the Zombie, the ability to develop into a Master networker simply lies dormant. What Zombies most need is to be taught, encouraged, and mentored. They need to be given information that increases awareness and opportunities. Then it is up to them to progress. It is not that Zombies have a "bad" attitude; their problem is that they lack mental focus. The Zombie can move upward and onward by adopting a learning attitude and making it a point to enter situations where learning naturally occurs: taking classes, reading books, and gleaning information and wisdom from others.

In charting their progress toward greater networking mastery, Zombies should focus on the Power of Knowing You, the Power of Interdependence, the Power of Quality Connections, and the Power of Thinking Big.

THE ROBOT

Robot networkers have good networking skills. They are well programmed to do the right things. They are organized and focused. Yet there's something missing: heart. Their interactions with people are correct but mechanical. Somehow they are too perfect, too pat, a bit rehearsed.

People with a Robot networking style typically attend conventions or conferences very focused and prepared. They make sure that they have their business cards handy; they have carefully reviewed the schedule of events and arrive at each session with notepad and pen in hand. They take voluminous notes, paying attention to every word of the presentation. In the process, they often miss out on opportunities to generate small talk with the people who are standing or sitting close by. Even when they do take the time to talk to people, it is mainly through pat responses and mechanical conversation, paying little attention to listening and connecting.

Robots almost always appear to be in charge of their life and their career. Everything is organized, from their résumé to their business card file to their schedule for the months ahead. However, they send their résumés out en masse, never realizing that it is the personal phone call or human connection that will create the quickest job opportunity. They have all the right answers for the interviewer, yet they miss the opportunity to come across with a sincere human touch.

The advantage of this style is the strong skills and good networking habits that Robots have already developed. The main weakness of Robots is that they lack a positive, supportive attitude. Their attitude toward other people tends to be "Don't waste my time," "I know what's best," "I'm busy; get to the point," and "I can do this myself." Robots have a tendency to run over people rather than include them. It would benefit the Robot to develop the following attitudes: "People are important in my life and to my success," "When I listen and show an interest in others we connect and then network more effectively," and "I can allow myself to have feelings and an interest in people without sacrificing my efficiency and success."

If you tend to have a Robot networking style, you can become a Master networker by focusing on relating. You must balance your need for perfection and results with an ability to connect with people and to be perceptive to others' needs. You must develop some sensitivity to go along with your discipline, and some human warmth to go along with your efficiency. The Power Principles to focus on include the Power of Praise, the Power of Quality Connections, the Power of Giving, and the Power of Listening.

THE SLOUCH

Slouch networkers have the right attitude regarding networking, yet they lack the impetus to do what it takes to develop the habits that would make the difference. Slouches often sound good, but after a while their words begin to lack credibility. They must add more substance to their networking by developing their abilities in several directions: improving their memory, being organized, staying on track, following up and following through.

Slouches can get excited about the opportunities in joining clubs and associations but only show up half the time. Because they lack focus, their conversations are often ineffective. In their excitement they tend to forget things and get sidetracked.

The strength of the Slouch style is a positive, supportive attitude. The positive attitude of Slouch networkers is embodied in such thoughts as "I have value to offer people," "People enjoy hearing from me," and "I value and appreciate the people in my support system." They exhibit a spirit of enthusiasm, awe, appreciation, and discovery. Slouches relate to people easily and quickly, but their networking power is impeded by wishful thinking, lack of discipline, even laziness.

Slouches tend to have a positive attitude about work but sometimes forget to plan ahead. They are content with their current skills rather than making sure they keep up with their personal and professional development. They naively think their career will progress naturally, without taking the initiative to continually plan their success and manage their career development.

To get on the course to mastery and stay there, Slouches need to especially focus on these Power Principles: the Power of Staying in Touch, the Power of Small Talk, the Power of Speaking Up, the Power of Asking, and the Power of Commitment.

THE DABBLER

The Dabbler is a person who networks in a haphazard manner. Dabblers have a good blend of attitudes and habits, yet they are still developing a full range of habits and their commitment is not fully entrenched. They are learning good networking skills and have turned some of those skills into habits, but they network more as a response to opportunities than by taking a powerful proactive approach. Their interest in networking is intermittent rather than integrated into everything they do. Their commitment and focus are sporadic rather than solid and consistent.

Dabblers may attend conventions with good intentions but they easily get sidetracked. Because their focus and preparation are haphazard, they miss out on some of the sessions that would best serve them. They may attend lots of meetings and be very aware of the opportunities available through networking clubs and professional associations, but they scatter their energy by participating in too many events, never making a commitment to the one or two groups that they could really penetrate and get great, long-lasting value from.

Dabblers tend to also be a little haphazard about their career. When they find themselves looking for a job, they have to take time to rebuild some of their network, as opposed to the Master, whose network is strong, up-to-date, and immediately accessible. Dabblers call people when they have a particular need, but they also must develop the habit of staying in touch with people simply for the sake of maintaining contact. Rather than using their networks for immediate gratification, they need to strengthen their long-term view to generate a support system that enhances their career over their lifetime.

As a Dabbler, your special strength is having a blend of the attitudes and habits that are instrumental in developing mastery. These attitudes include a strong sense of self and an appreciation for other people. You are already aware of the opportunities available through building relationships and working together in a support system. You have developed the ability to make small talk lead to results and the confidence to speak up in a positive manner. You know how to ask and get things to happen.

Dabblers already value the results that can happen through networking. They just need to develop a strong sense of the value that a masterful networking life-style holds for them. They would benefit from adopting attitudinal mottoes like "Networking is important enough in my life to be a priority," "I am networking for the long term," and "I am com-

153

mitted to having a strong, lifetime network that serves me and everyone in my support system." By developing a passion from within, they can grow to be more proactive, drawing on a sense of self-generated power.

If you fit the Dabbler style, your approach to networking is catch-as-catch-can. You are on the road to mastering the twelve Power Principles, but you are not there yet. Intention, focus, and discipline would catapult you to mastery. The Power Principles to focus on include the Power of Giving, the Power of Interdependence, the Power of Thinking Big, and—most important of all—the Power of Commitment.

THE MASTER

The Master is the proficient networker who has developed a networking style that is natural, effective, and mutually supportive. Master networkers have integrated and incorporated all the skills and attitudes embodied in the twelve Power Principles into their very existence. They don't consciously think about how to network; they find themselves asking, offering, listening, responding.

Masters can attend a conference or convention, have a great time, meet lots of interesting people, and generate lots of new opportunities. It seems that business opportunities miraculously show up wherever they go. They encounter substantially more opportunities than others, while having seemingly done less to make them happen. However, they know how to prepare themselves for these events, and they have worked to develop their ability to approach people, to generate conversations, to listen, to offer help, and to be responsive. They always have their business cards and pen handy, and when an opportunity arises to exchange information, they do so in a gracious, professional manner.

If you are already a Master networker, you have an attitude of self-confidence and appreciation for others, and you have cultivated habits that will support a networking life-style for a lifetime. Masters know the importance of choosing where to spend their time and energy. Rather than dispersing their energy like the Dabbler, they focus it on the people they are with and the organizations they have chosen to participate in.

Master networkers realize the importance of networking for networking's sake. Rather than waiting for times of need, they work to maintain their network during the up times as well as the downs. When they want to make a job or career change they have lots of people they have stayed in touch with over the years whom they can call on for information and support. They know they are in charge of their own career and value networking as their most important career management tool.

Masters fully understand the big picture of networking and the value of building a lifetime support system. They trust the big picture enough to be focused on giving to others and watching for opportunities. Master networkers have practiced the skills of networking to the point where their implementation is natural, consistent, and effective.

LEARNING TO BE A MASTER

155

Choosing to grow involves taking conscious steps to shift your attitudes, develop new habits, recondition your thinking, and implement new behaviors. According to George Leonard, author of *Mastery: The Keys to Success and Long-Term Fulfillment,* the term *mastery* "resists definition yet can be instantly recognized. . . . It brings rich rewards, yet is not really a goal or a destination but rather a process, a journey." He emphasizes that "mastery isn't reserved for the super-talented or even for those who are fortunate enough to have gotten an early start. It's available to anyone who is willing to get on the path and stay on it." The journey to mastery starts whenever you choose to get on the path.

Mastering the art of networking will not happen overnight. It takes time, practice, and persistence. However, the journey toward mastery can start right now. It's up to you to take action and start yourself on an exciting journey of discovery and development. It is the blend of your awareness, attitudes, habits, and skills that constitutes your ability to relate to your world from a sense of power, strength, and satisfaction. Finding the proper balance of attitudes and habits is the basis for being masterful at the art of networking. And it is as a Master networker that you will discover the joy of having a support system that continually enriches your life.

CHAPTER SEVENTEEN

RECONDITIONING YOURSELF FOR SUCCESS

"Take charge of your thoughts and do what you will with them."

—Plato

NETWORKING IS A VERY NATURAL PROCESS: it is about friendship, caring, sharing, and supporting people, none of which are difficult or unnatural. Yet many people feel uncomfortable asking for help, offering support, or meeting new people. Why does networking sometimes feel so unnatural, uncomfortable, and difficult? Typically, it is simply because we have not done it before. Riding a bicycle probably felt awkward to you on your first try, but now you probably think nothing of it. Networking is similar. Through the process of "getting on the bike" or, in this case, networking and developing positive interpersonal skills and habits, you will discover the ease and thrill of "riding the bike." Some people just seem to be natural networkers—they must have been born that way. The Olympic gold medal winners also seem to be naturals at what they do—they appear to have been born with their ability.

Yet most of them have spent the majority of their life training, practicing, and developing their ability until it looks and feels easy and natural!

Can anyone learn to network? I have worked with top executives, sales representatives, homemakers, machinery operators, CPAs, attorneys, nurses, real estate agents, and insurance agents, and they have all learned to be effective with their networking. Some people who are very quiet and laid-back are powerful networkers because they are very good listeners, they pay attention to people, and they place a high value on friendships. Others who are very outgoing and energetic are strong, effective networkers because they meet people easily, draw people to them with their enthusiasm, and are quick to respond to the opportunities around them. Whatever your style and personality, you can develop your strengths to create a networking style that is easy, natural, and effective for you.

However, some obstacles usually stand in the way of effective networking. We have fears that have been reinforced by failures or rejections in the past, and we have developed certain thoughts about what's appropriate and inappropriate. We all have beliefs that have influenced us all our lives, based on the things we heard, read, and experienced as we were growing up. I am going to refer to this as conditioning. We are conditioned by society, by our upbringing, by loved ones, by our gender, our class, and many other factors. Each of us grew up in an environment that contributed to the way we view ourselves and relate to others.

Everything around you has contributed to your beliefs, your style, your mode of operation, your attitude, your thought processes—in short, your conditioning. This conditioning becomes accepted as truth and therefore becomes the way that you unconsciously live and operate in the world. However, you can reevaluate your conditioning and reestablish the way you respond to and live your life. Some of your conditioning may support and some of it may hinder your networking effectiveness. Strengthening your networking power starts with understanding your conditioning so that you can recondition yourself to learn and practice new attitudes and skills.

WERE YOU TOLD . . . ?

The following seven types of conditioning can influence your networking effectiveness without your even realizing it. Review them to see which ones you relate to and decide how you would like to develop more positive and effective conditioning.

"Don't Talk to Strangers"

This is wise advice, especially when you are young and vulnerable and haven't developed sufficient discernment. However, as adults we can and must allow ourselves to make contact with the people around us. Someone once said, "A stranger is just someone I haven't met yet." Talking to people you haven't met yet can be a gold mine of opportunities. Sometimes chance meetings or passing comments will open the door to conversations that lead to new jobs, new friendships, or new clients.

"Be Strong"

Strength is a positive quality when it is related to mental vitality, emotional strength, or physical ability. However, some people think being strong means not asking for help, doing everything on their own, and being other people's savior or hero. Being strong does not mean being stoic, isolated, or unapproachable. We are strong in spirit when we occasionally allow ourselves to have uncomfortable feelings. We are strong mentally when we can sort through our options and clarify what we want, identify the resources we need, and then take the steps to get there. We are strong in our sense of self when we are comfortable acknowledging others' strength enough to include them without feeling threatened. Be strong in your resolve to call on your network, realizing that asking for help is a sign, not of weakness, but of maturity and strength.

"Be a Big Boy—or a Big Girl"

Being childlike isn't the same as being childish. When children are told to be "big," they begin to relate being grown-up to being serious, not having feelings, or not having fun. The enthusiasm of a child is a great character trait at any age. As we grow in physical stature, we hope to grow in wisdom while retaining some of the childlike traits that enrich life. Ideally, networking should include a childlike enthusiasm for life; great feelings of caring, interest, warmth, and satisfaction; and lots of fun!

"You Can't Trust Others"

We can all think of situations where we could justifiably choose to never again trust men, women, our parents, our children, rich people, lawyers, salespeople, and so on. However, a life of not trusting is not much of a life. It can be very difficult to recover from betrayed trust. When we trust someone, it is often a devastating and painful blow to find out our trust was misplaced. We can easily generalize our feelings of caution and mistrust and project our mistrust on people who actually can be trusted. Learn to bring into your network people who are worthy of your trust. Trust is a major element of a strong relationship. The more trust you develop with the people in your support system, the greater the value of the networking that takes place.

161

"Don't Bother That Person"

If you were ever told not to bother your father, your mother, the teacher, Uncle Harry, or Grandma, that thought may have been internalized as "You are a bother" or "What you want is not important" or "Others are more important." Imagine if you had been spoken to in another way: "Mother is busy finishing a proposal for a client right now. However, I know she plans to finish within the next hour and then you can show her all your beautiful drawings." Or what if instead of "Don't bother me. Can't you see I'm busy?" you heard, "I know you want some attention right now, but I need some time to finish what I'm doing. If you'll play with your toys for a while, as soon as I finish we'll play together for an hour before you go to bed." People are only a bother when they are selfish or inappropriate with their words, timing, actions, or behaviors. It is not a bother to call on people. People want to contribute and you can call on them in such a way that they feel acknowledged and included.

"Don't Depend on Others"

You may have been told, "You shouldn't depend on others" or "You'd better learn to take care of yourself." To depend on someone simply means to trust or rely on them. I obviously have to depend on others to do the many things that I can't do—repair my car, build my home, fly the airplane, upgrade the computer. I depend on these people to add to my life by doing what they do well. I obviously trust these people because I fly on their plane, I allow them to repair my car, I buy their computer.

It is important to develop your own sense of self-value, self-worth, and self-love. If you look to or depend on others for your happiness, success, or love, you will also tend to blame others for your disappointments. When you blame others, you never get the chance to experience your own power in life. However, once you have that core experience of self-love and self-value, you can look to others to enrich what you already have in life.

"Don't Let Yourself Be Hurt"

Have you been told, "If you don't depend on others, you can't be let down" or "If you aren't vulnerable, you can't be hurt" or "If you don't give of yourself, you can't be used"? What kind of a life would this be if we couldn't count on others to be there, if we couldn't give without worrying about a return? I think everyone would agree—it wouldn't be much of a life. No matter what you do, you can't protect yourself so that you never feel hurt, disappointed, or misunderstood. Mistakes happen, human error happens, misunderstandings happen. We all wish they didn't, and when they do, we can only hope we've learned from the experience. But that doesn't mean there won't be other disappointments. We're dealing with human nature and variables that are beyond our control.

When you give of yourself freely, you cannot be used. You run the risk of feeling used when you give more than you can afford to give, either financially, mentally, or emotionally, and you expect and need something in return. Give only what you can afford to give and feel good about giving. This is where we all must take care of ourselves because we are the only ones who know our own limits. No one else can know how much we can afford to give and still feel full within ourselves.

Don't set yourself up for disappointment by approaching people who don't want to be supportive. Don't go to a drill sergeant if what you need is a nurse. Go to a drill sergeant when you need focus and discipline. Go to a nurse when you need healing and comforting. Go to people who are likely to have what you need or to be able to respond to what you are asking. Don't imagine that people are going to be any different than they are. Don't show your vulnerabilities to someone

163

 Recondition Yourself for Success

Answer the following questions to identify the reconditioning that will lead you to even greater success:

What conditioning am I now aware of?

How has this conditioning affected my success?

What changes (reconditioning) do I want to make?

who has no compassion and expect that person to be compassionate. If you know people who tend to be gruff, insensitive, and rude, don't be surprised when they are. If approaching them is worth dealing with the gruff, insensitive behavior, then do so knowing what you are getting into.

Bring the kind of people into your network who want to network. Develop relationships with those who are willing to allow the relationship to be mutually supportive.

Recondition Yourself:

☑ Trust people who are trustworthy.

☑ Feel the strength and maturity that it takes to ask for and accept support and assistance.

☑ Enjoy the childlike qualities of enthusiasm, awe, appreciation, and discovery.

☑ Relate to each person individually—don't project an unpleasant experience with one person to all people of that gender, industry, race, or creed.

☑ Accept someone's busyness without taking it personally.

☑ Develop your own sense of confidence and self-esteem.

IT'S UP TO YOU

The more aware you are of how you were conditioned to think and relate and respond to others, the greater your ability will be to make positive changes in your networking style. Reconditioning yourself is not necessarily easy, yet it can be the most empowering, freeing, and loving thing you can do for yourself. Conditioning that has been ingrained and adhered to for many years does not change overnight. However, with great awareness, commitment, and persistence, you can condition yourself in the way that you choose!

CHAPTER EIGHTEEN

CHOOSING NEW HABITS
FOR LIFETIME RESULTS

*" **W**e are what we repeatedly do.*
Excellence, then, is not an act, but a habit. "

—Aristotle

HOW DO YOU CHANGE the conditioning that has been part of your whole life? The best way is patiently and gently, yet with persistence. To change the conditioning that keeps you from meeting people, developing strong contacts, and building a nurturing support system, you must become aware of what you want to change. You can get rid of the old habits or attitudes by identifying and beginning to focus on the new ones. Through your willingness to let go, shed that old familiar skin, and grow a new one, you can begin to implement your new habits. With persistence, patience, determination, and discipline, you will find yourself developing a new you.

Think about all the ideas in this book as habits. Notice how you get in the habit of thinking a certain way, behaving in a certain way, responding to people in a certain way, and acting a particular way in certain situations. Many of your actions, behaviors, and thought patterns are simply habits you have developed over time. Your thoughts lead to actions and behaviors. At the same time, your actions and behaviors can support the development of a certain mindset. To truly make changes in your life, you must address your thoughts, actions, and behaviors.

By definition, a habit is automatic. It is anything you do for a period of time until it becomes so natural that you do it without thinking. Because habits are automatic, they can be deeply ingrained, but it is important to remember that you can practice a new behavior until it becomes automatic and, thus, a new habit.

The process of developing habits has three steps:

1. Have awareness and a desire to change.
2. Choose new actions, attitudes, and behaviors.
3. Focus on and implement your new habits.

HAVE AWARENESS AND A DESIRE TO CHANGE

167

Awareness is the first step to implementing new behaviors, thought patterns, and habits. When you become aware that you are doing or saying something you don't like, you can start to think about what you would like to do or say differently. It is only through awareness that you can change your behavior. It is the start of your growth process.

Learning is an ongoing process. The "mistakes," the tough times, and the difficulties often teach us the most about what we want and the changes we must make to have what we want. In the popular animated Disney movie *The Lion King,* the wise monkey, Rafiki, teaches Simba about learning by hitting him over the head with his staff. Simba is surprised that Rafiki would hit him for no reason. However, a moment later, when Rafiki makes the same swing with his staff toward Simba's head, Simba stops the blow with his mighty paw. Rafiki nods with pleasure, reminding Simba that past hurts and mistakes are opportunities to learn. We are more able to maintain a mental state of power, strength, and acceptance when we view life as learning opportunities that will help us to grow spiritually, mentally, and professionally.

New awareness quickly leads to the "Ah-ha!" stage, in which we realize that there is a new way, although we are still playing out the old habit. This is a difficult stage, so it is important to remind yourself that you are making progress even when that progress is not as fast as you would like. As you maintain your awareness and persistence, you will reach the point where you begin to exhibit the new behavior.

CHOOSE NEW ACTIONS, ATTITUDES, AND BEHAVIORS

After you become aware of what you want to change, you must decide what new actions, attitudes, and behaviors you want in your life. Old habits don't just go away, and new habits don't suddenly appear. Making a change means replacing the old with something new. It takes attention, effort, and consistency. However, with a little effort, the reward for a short period of focused attention will be reaped continually over a long period of time.

Which of these thoughts or actions are habits of yours? Think about how they serve you.

- Do you stay too busy to "stop and smell the roses," or do you send acknowledgment notes on a regular basis?

- Do you commonly forget people's names, or do you pay attention when people introduce themselves, repeating their names to remember them?

- Do you usually try to do things on your own, or do you easily and regularly call people for support and assistance?

- Do you procrastinate about calling people, or do you stay in touch with people through regular phone calls?

- Do you retreat when things get tough, or do you call on your close friends for comfort, encouragement, and understanding?

- Do you misplace your business cards and lose track of information, or are you using a computer program to help you to keep track of information and have access to it?

Since habits lead to results, you must develop the habits that lead to the results you desire. At a young age, we get in the habit of brushing our teeth, which then becomes an automatic part of our daily routine. This habit leads to healthy teeth and gums. If I have a new book idea, it is important that I get in the habit of writing on a regular basis. And if I want an active network, it is important that I get in the habit of calling people and sending notes on a regular basis.

Every year, I select a couple of habits to focus on during the year; I know that by the end of the year I will have made a shift in my attitude, action, or behaviors. I also have the satisfaction of knowing that every year I am taking steps to continue my own personal and professional development by reviewing old habits and developing new ones.

FOCUS ON YOUR NEW HABITS

169

The combination of awareness and action generates new habits. However, it is important to remember that learning takes practice. Do you remember when you first learned the multiplication tables, a new language, the state capitals? You had to repeat the information over and over. Do you remember when you first learned to ride a bike, or skate, or ski? You needed help getting on that bike and staying balanced, until at some magical moment you had it! And then you never lost it.

When networking becomes the natural and automatic way we relate and interact, then we've developed the networking habit. Imagine what that would be like: we would spontaneously acknowledge the people around us; we would ask, "What can I do for you?" at the end of all phone calls; we would easily and regularly ask for support for our goals and dreams; we would respond to that intuitive urge to call someone; and we would offer information, support, or contacts to most of the people we met.

WHAT DO YOU WANT?

It is helpful to define what you want, then to list a habit that you can develop to help you reach that goal:

What I Want:	Action That Supports What I Want:
To triple my sales	Call three new prospects (a day, a week)
To reconnect with people I've lost touch with	Call one person a week whom I haven't talked to in a long time
To be rested, healthy, and available to my network	Get eight hours of sleep per night
To nurture those relationships that enrich my life	Talk to a friend every day
To stay aware of my dreams and goals	Write in my journal
To become known in my industry	Have a business lunch with an associate once a week
To be more comfortable meeting people	Say hello or generate conversation with someone new
To be more comfortable calling on my support system	Ask someone for assistance or feedback weekly
To be a better listener	Give someone my undivided attention
To have satisfied clients who stay as clients for the long term	Call clients just to say hi!
To be more effective with getting to know people quickly	Listen and ask open-ended questions

You become your habits—those you've developed consciously and those you've slipped into unconsciously. Your power as a human being comes with your ability to notice and become aware of your patterns and mold yourself into the person you want to be!

THE COURAGE TO CHANGE

It takes not only awareness, focus, and consistency to develop new habits; it also takes courage to make changes that will affect your life, your business, your sense of self, and your relationships. In *Further Along the Road Less Traveled,* Scott Peck observes: "Most people think that courage is the absence of fear." Courage is not the absence of fear, he says. "Courage is the willingness to take steps in the presence of fear." We can never guarantee an absence of fear as we grow, learn, and explore new aspects of ourselves. So when we experience fear, discomfort, or concern about making certain changes, that's okay.

The fear that accompanies change is natural and understandable. Notice your feelings and move forward. Pick a new behavior or thought pattern and focus on it every day. Start now and before you know it you will have a new, positive, productive habit that enhances your networking life-style!

171

 New Habits for Success

Answer the following questions to identify the habits that would be most beneficial in your life:

What are my productive and supportive habits?

What habits do I have that are detrimental and counterproductive?

What new habits would serve me?

WHAT WILL YOU DO TODAY?

Often, the hardest part of developing a new habit is getting started. Here are some actions you can take right away:

Send a note to someone who has inspired you in your profession.

Call a friend whom you haven't talked to recently.

Ask for help.

Take a few moments to appreciate your life.

Do one thing that you have been putting off doing.

Introduce yourself to someone you don't know.

Offer support to someone in your family.

Send a surprise gift to a client or colleague.

PART

IV

POLISHING YOUR
NETWORKING
SKILLS

10 NETWORKING TURNOFFS AND HOW TO AVOID THEM

One's philosophy is not best expressed in words. It is expressed in the choices one makes. And the choices we make are ultimately our responsibility.

—Eleanor Roosevelt

NETWORKING IS OFTEN GIVEN A bad reputation because people misuse the concept in a way that is inconsiderate, inappropriate, unprofessional, or shortsighted. These people may not even be aware of what they are doing that turns people off and creates a negative impression. Just as little things can have a positive impact on our relationships, little things that we do inappropriately can ruin our chances for developing strong networking relationships. The following ten scenarios outline common networking turnoffs.

1. Coming on too strong

Coming on too strong and trying to sell too soon is a turnoff to most people. You must invest the time to get to know people and find out what they need. Networking involves learning about other people—their interests, goals, dreams, and hobbies. The more you know about them, the more likely you are to find reasons to introduce them to the expertise and services you offer.

Selling to your network doesn't have to be a problem. You can approach people to introduce yourself, your products, and your services without turning them off. The best way is to focus on people, listen to them, give to them, and show a natural interest in them. Through selling yourself first and investing in relationships, you will find that people are more likely to respond with trust, and their interest in networking with you and buying from you will grow.

2. Being insincere

177

Have you ever felt that people were giving you a lead just to look good or were saying that they would do something when they had no intention of following through? Networking must be sincere and authentic to inspire a strong, trusting level of relationship. The masterful networker realizes that networking is not about looking good or immediate gratification, but about building a support system for a lifetime. The way to do this is by providing quality leads and following up with people because you truly care. People who name-drop or pretend an interest are not showing the authenticity that leads to good networking. The quality of your networking is directly related to the sincerity of your interactions.

3. Making idle promises

Many people habitually say, "Let's get together" or "Let's do lunch." The comment is made spontaneously with little if any actual thought of follow-through. If you do not intend to follow through, the statement is insincere and ineffective. I broke myself of this habit by promising myself that I wouldn't say it unless I really meant it, and if I meant it, I would say, "Let's schedule lunch. Are you available on . . . ?" Make the most of your interactions by making statements that generate positive actions.

4. Being rude

Have you had people introduce themselves, spend a minute finding out what you do, and then quickly drop you when they realize you are not a prospect for their business? What a terrible feeling and missed opportunity—to approach someone as a "piece of business" rather than a valued person. It is rude, unprofessional, and inappropriate to think of networking events as business "meat markets." They are a place to meet people, make contacts, reconnect with people, and gather information. People are much more than potential clients. Someone who does not even look like a prospect could turn out to be one of the most valuable contacts you could ever make, but not if you don't take the time to learn a little bit about that person, develop the first stepping-stone of a relationship, and treat the person with common courtesy.

5. Being too focused on sales

Have you ever been to a networking event where you felt as if you were the target of a sales representative whose only focus was to make a sale or schedule an appointment? A person whose total focus is to make a sale misses out on connecting with people and instead conveys an attitude that turns people off. Networking events are not the place to "sell." Nurture your contacts; ask for the opportunity to follow up with a phone call, but don't put people on the spot. I appreciate the drive, determination, and focus it takes to be a successful salesperson. However, I prefer to interact with salespeople who know and understand the difference between networking and selling. Remember that sales don't come first; people do!

6. Not paying attention

Have you ever talked to someone who constantly scanned the room to see who else was there? If you give someone your undivided attention for even one minute, that person will notice and remember you. It doesn't have to take long to connect with someone, but it will never happen if you are too busy trying to make sure that you connect with everyone rather than connecting with the person who is right in front of you.

7. Monopolizing the conversation

Have you ever been cornered by someone who talks so incessantly that you feel hopelessly trapped? A conversation is meant to be an interaction between two or more people. Yet some people can talk on and on without realizing that they have monopolized the conversation. When people get carried away with their own conversation, you will have to get their attention long enough to break in. If a soft approach doesn't work, you will have to be firm. Some people don't know how to listen, to engage in a two-way conversation, or to include others. When this is the case, you must take charge. Ways to intercede in or conclude a conversation include: "Sorry to interrupt, but I do need to speak to some other people here before they leave. Good luck with the project you're talking about," or "Excuse me. I know I'm changing the subject, but I wanted to talk for a minute about . . ."

179

8. Being impersonal with business cards

Have you ever been handed a business card when you've never even had a chance to talk to or get to know the person? The exchange of business cards is best done one-on-one once some rapport has been established. Typically, you will reach a point in your conversation where it is natural to ask for or offer a card. When you are handed a card, take a moment to look at it. Looking at the card conveys respect and helps with memory recall. This is also the opportunity to make sure you understand all of the information on the card. If you ask for a card, explain why you want it: "I would like to send you some information about my presentation so you can consider me for your next conference," or "I know someone I think it would be good for you to call. If you'll give me a card, I'll make a note to call you with her name and number."

9. Interrupting

Have you ever been answering someone's question only to be interrupted with another question or comment before you have finished what you were saying? Our minds get so busy that it may be hard at times to slow down and really listen. However, delighted attention and sincere listening make people notice at a subconscious level. People want to be listened to. They want to be heard. Giving them your attention for even a short period of time will greatly enhance their chances of remembering you for a long time.

10. Exaggerating and embellishing

You don't have to feel as if you are risking your reputation or putting yourself on the line by referring someone. When you network you are simply passing along information in a way that allows other people to be responsible for any decisions they make. There is no need to embellish or speak for someone else. You never know for sure if two people are going to "click" or not; however, you can be the conveyer of information that helps them find what they are looking for.

How Not to Exaggerate Your Connections

Don't guarantee someone else's services:

"Call Carol. She'll give you the lowest price in town."

Instead, convey the information you have:

"Carol sells computers and computer accessories. I heard her say that she typically can beat almost any other price in town."

Don't speak for someone else:

"John will take good care of you."

Instead, speak from your experience:

"John has always taken good care of my travel needs. I've been using him for three years and have been very pleased."

Don't exaggerate:

"Harry is the best there ever was."

Instead, give a realistic basis for your recommendation:

"Harry is the best I've ever come across. He was able to . . . I highly recommend him."

181

Don't oversell:

"You've got to use Jan. She does exactly what you're looking for. She's perfect for you! Here, I'll call her right now and you can talk to her!"

Instead, offer to support in whatever way best suits people:

"I know someone who sounds like a perfect fit for what you're looking for and I think you two would work well together. Here's her number. Please use my name, and if you would like me to call her or assist in any way I'll be glad to."

Networking DO's

Networking is an attitude of partnership and contribution. It is an approach to life based on cooperation, and it is a way of interacting with people in a spirit of relationship. Networking is about serving and supporting others. When we network one step at a time, one day at a time, we are building a foundation of support that lasts for a lifetime.

- ☑ Focus on people so that you remember their name.

- ☑ Wear your name tag on the upper right side of your jacket or dress so that it is easy for people to see.

- ☑ Reintroduce yourself to people you haven't seen in a while or don't know well.

- ☑ Organize your network list for easy recall.

- ☑ Practice active listening to ensure clear communication.

- ☑ Listen more than you talk.

- ☑ Call people you have not seen or talked to in a long time.

- ☑ Be proactive in offering information to others with no strings attached.

- ☑ Praise yourself and others daily.

- ☑ Inspire others as a role model for professional networking.

- ☑ Use your network as a stepping-stone to reach people.

- ☑ Practice the "Golden Rule of Networking": Give unto others as you would have them give unto you.

- ☑ Focus on building the kind of relationships that you want for a lifetime. Be patient, yet persistent, with your networking.

- ☑ Use your business card as your calling card.

- ☑ Ask for what you want in a way that acknowledges and includes others.

15 WAYS TO MAKE THE MOST OF EVERY NETWORKING OPPORTUNITY

*" **The** key to our species' success is our great skill in making close alliances with others. "*

—William F. Allman

CHAMBER OF COMMERCE ACTIVI-TIES, business open houses, confer-ences, trade shows, conventions, association meetings—all of these are networking events, and all of them can be fun, productive, and valuable opportunities. Or, as many people have experienced, they can be uncomfortable, time-consuming, and unproductive. Making good use of networking events involves choosing the right events for your interests and developing a person-able approach for meeting people.

Many organizations exist that provide positive and powerful net-working opportunities for their members. Professional associa-tions tend to represent one specific type of industry and are therefore an excellent resource for knowledge, information, and contacts. They can help to establish you in your industry, keep you in touch with your peers, and provide educational programs for your profession.

A particularly valuable resource for business owners is the networking club or entrepreneurial support group. These groups meet regularly and include business owners from various industries. Ivan Misner, in *The World's Best-Known Marketing Secret,* refers to these groups as "strong-contact networks" because they provide "highly focused opportunities" for you to develop a word-of-mouth marketing support system.

Richard Weylman, in *Opening Closed Doors,* tells us that "one of the most effective ways to become well known and achieve high visibility is to meet your prospects face-to-face at their clubs, association meetings and social functions." To make the most of your networking potential, you have to join and have a presence in organizations that place you in front of the people who can either buy from you or network with you.

MINGLE LIKE A MASTER

185

"There won't be anyone to talk to."

"I won't fit in."

"I won't know what to say."

"People won't remember me."

"I'll be dressed wrong for the event."

"Everyone will be trying to sell me something."

"I don't like small talk."

"I'm not good at small talk."

Most people feel somewhat uncomfortable walking into a roomful of people they don't know. However, through preparation you can develop your ability to mingle with ease, have a good time, and calm those networking jitters. Here are fifteen ideas to help you prepare for these events and enjoy yourself while you're there.

1. Learn what you need to know

Everything you need to know about the event may be on the invitation. What type of event is it? Is it a sit-down meal, a buffet, a trade show with exhibits and seminars, a more intimate open house? Will you be introducing yourself to people one-on-one or will you be asked to stand and introduce yourself to the whole group? Who are the probable attendees? How long will it last? How much time will it take?

Think about what will make you feel most comfortable. Would you prefer to get there early and already be in the room as others are arriving? Would you like to arrive later so that you can walk in feeling that things are already happening? Would you feel more comfortable arriving with someone else? Can you call someone else who is going and attend together? Is it the type of event where you could bring a friend or associate? If so, who from your network would it be appropriate to invite? (This is a way to include others from your network, spend some time with them, and offer them an opportunity that could be of value to them.) If you do decide to go with someone else, make sure you don't use that as an excuse to avoid talking to others. You and your friend might make an agreement to mingle for twenty minutes, then touch base with each other, and then mingle some more. Or you might mingle together, introducing your friend to the people you know. Or you might each go off on your own and set a certain time to meet and leave, then go somewhere to visit and talk.

2. Identify what you want to accomplish and the people you want to talk to

You can have many reasons for attending an event. You may have been working so hard that it would be good simply to give yourself a break, get away from the office, and enjoy being with others. You may know that someone you've been wanting to meet is going to be there. It may be a good opportunity to stay visible, reconnect with people you already know, and make some new contacts. Or you may be interested in the organization that's sponsoring the event and see the event as a chance to get to know more about the organization and meet its members. The more you are aware of your reasons, the easier it will be to make sure that you accomplish what you want.

Think about who is likely to be at the event and make a mental note of those with whom you'd like to talk. This is an opportunity to reconnect with people and make new contacts, learn more about others, gather information, and strengthen your relationships while at the same time expanding your network.

3. Think about how you want to present yourself

At some events, you introduce yourself individually to people in a mix-and-mingle environment, while at others, you introduce yourself to the whole group. Think about the introduction you developed for yourself in Chapter Twelve. By thinking ahead about how you want to present yourself, you will feel better prepared and therefore more comfortable. You will also display more clarity and confidence, which enhances your ability to generate conversation, put others at ease, and create stronger connections with people. Present yourself in a positive and professional manner. Speak with confidence regarding the value and benefit of who you are and what you have to offer.

4. Think about what you can say to initiate conversations that generate rapport

By thinking ahead and becoming mentally prepared, you can be comfortable and effective approaching people and generating conversations. If you feel uncomfortable with the small talk aspect of networking, remember that you always have something in common with those who are at the same event. Look for something of interest to talk about. Ask open-

187

ended questions or make general statements that invite responses. Listen and show a natural interest in people. If you're not trying to obtain a particular result, you can allow yourself to simply enjoy the interaction.

At networking events it is valuable to be able to connect with people easily and establish rapport quickly. You establish rapport by sharing something in common, exchanging information, or showing an interest. When you do this you will find people responding to you with warmth and openness.

5. Have your networking supplies handy

Networking calls for business cards, pens, brochures, note cards, and a date planner. The essential supplies for a networking event are your business cards and a pen for making notes on those cards. Everyone should have business cards. They are your calling card, the tool used for sharing information and letting others know how to contact you. Whether you're a business owner, a clerical support person, a student, a full-time parent, or a job seeker, a business card assures you of being able to share essential information with others in an easy, effective manner.

One of my contacts at one of the big-six CPA firms that I conduct trainings for left the company and decided to take some time off before she pursued her next career step. I had not talked to her since she left the company when I saw her at a mutual friend's birthday party. After we talked and caught up on each other's activities, I told her I would like to know how to be in touch with her. She quickly and easily responded by handing me a very nice personal calling card that had her name, address, and phone number in script lettering on ivory card stock. Susan was prepared. She knew the value of networking and presenting herself in a professional manner at all times. Make sure you always have your business cards and a pen handy so that you can find them easily to make notes on the follow-through you promise the people you meet.

6. Take charge of your participation

It is up to you. You can take a passive approach, wanting and hoping people will approach you. Or you can be proactive and approach the people you want to talk to, thus taking an active role in making the event a success. Some people feel more comfortable at an event if they have a "job" to do such as greeting people, handling registration, or serving refreshments. If having something to do helps you to feel more comfortable, then volunteer your services. Another idea is to mentally take on the role of being a host for the event. Being a host involves greeting people, making sure they are taken care of, and introducing them to one another. Anything you do to help the event flow well and be successful will actually benefit you as well.

7. Be people-focused rather than self-focused

Rather than worrying about what you're going to say, focus on what others are saying. When you give people your attention you'll be more likely to remember them and they'll be more likely to remember and appreciate you. Concentrating your attention on something or someone other than yourself reduces your self-consciousness.

8. Listen

Show an interest in people by listening. Good conversationalists know the importance of listening. It helps you to become more aware of what to say and what to talk about in order to keep the conversation flowing in an easy, natural way.

9. Call people by their name

Pay attention as people introduce themselves so that you can repeat their name back to them and remember it for the future. It means a great deal to most people to have someone remember their name, both when you have just met them and when you can remember their name at a later date.

189

10. Exchange business cards when the time is right

Business cards are best exchanged during a conversation where there is some stated reason for the exchange, for example, "I'll call about scheduling a time to get together for lunch," or "Let me have your card and I'll send that information to you tomorrow," or "Here's my card. Call me if I can be of any help the next time you're in Houston."

11. Keep the flow going

A networking event is a place to meet and mingle, yet people often don't know how to end a conversation so that they can mingle and talk with others. There is no need to feel guilty or uncomfortable about wanting to end a conversation to talk with other people. Be gracious to the person you are talking with by making a closing comment such as "Nice to meet you. Have a good evening," or "Good luck with your new venture," or "Enjoyed talking with you. I hope to see you again at next month's meeting."

12. Use body language to connect and communicate

Body language is a very powerful means of communication at networking events. A slight turn of the shoulders or the body, a nod, a wave of the hand, or a glance with the eyes can be a signal that includes others and acknowledges their presence. Watch for a break in the conversation when you can either invite the person to join you, introduce the person, or include the person by asking a question that relates to the conversation: "John, we're talking about . . . You've probably dealt with that in your business," or "Amy, good to see you. Come join us. We're talking about . . . ," or "Everyone, I would like you to meet Matt. Matt does . . ."

At other times you will be the one wanting to join a group that is already involved in conversation. If you notice that people are very engrossed in a discussion, this may not be the right time to try to engage in conversation with them. You may want to find someone else to talk with and then approach them later. If you really want to be part of their conversation, stand close by and wait to see if someone will include you by using eye contact, body language, or a comment that acknowledges your presence and invites you into the conversation. Listen for an opening in the conversation where you can make an appropriate comment: "You're talking about the upcoming chamber expo. I just learned that they are looking for . . ." or "I heard you talking about the Internet. I read an article in this month's issue of . . . that was very helpful."

13. Relax, have fun, and enjoy yourself

Often people are nervous about attending networking events because they feel as if they have to find a new prospect, make a sale, or accomplish some significant goal. Networking is meant to be fun. Relax. The more comfortable you feel, the more comfortable others will feel around you and the more likely you will be to make good, solid contacts. Sometimes people get so results-oriented that they forget to slow down and just enjoy a simple conversation. Your goal should be to have quality interactions with the people you meet, rather than focusing on meeting a lot of people just for the sake of meeting a lot of people. It is much better to meet a few people who will remember you in a positive light the next day than to meet a lot of people who will not remember who you are or what you do.

191

14. Say thanks

Say thanks to the sponsors of the event and the people who invited you. Before leaving let the people who were responsible for organizing or sponsoring the event know you appreciate all the work they did to make the event a success. Be sure to let the person who invited you or was responsible for getting you on the invitation list know that you appreciate being included. A thank-you note to these people is also very appropriate.

15. Follow up

Prompt, effective follow-up is essential as reinforcement for the value that was generated through the contacts you made. The follow-up may be everything from sending thank-you notes or calling someone with the phone number of a contact you recommended, to sending a brochure or flyer, scheduling that lunch meeting you discussed, or calling to thank someone for attending and inviting them to the next meeting. Be sure to make notes regarding any follow-up activity that needs to be done in the future and make sure that the information you collected regarding the people you met and talked to is added into your data base. Immediate follow-up as you meet people makes a major difference in having people remember you and reinforces the possibility of networking now and in the future.

All networking opportunities have the potential to be positive, fun, and fruitful. It is up to you to make them positive and productive experiences. Allow yourself to relax and enjoy the fellowship that goes with meeting and talking to people. Eat and drink lightly and pace yourself. You can be focused and fulfill your purpose in attending and yet still allow things to happen easily. By following the principles and ideas in this book, you can leave any networking event feeling energized, enthusiastic, and encouraged.

Networking Event Prep Sheet

A little thought and preparation can have a big impact on your confidence and effectiveness when attending networking events. Prior to attending an event answer the following questions to get yourself mentally focused and prepared:

What do I need to know about the event (date, time, location, type of event, format, probable attendees)?

What do I want to accomplish by attending this event?

Who are the people I want to reconnect with at the event?

Who are the new people I want to meet at the event?

What topics of interest would be useful in talking with these people?

How do I plan to introduce myself?

What types of conversation initiators would be most helpful in putting others at ease?

193

12 QUESTIONS EVEN MASTER NETWORKERS ASK

66 ***A*** *noble person attracts noble people and knows how to hold on to them.* *99*

—Johann Wolfgang von Goethe

MASTER NETWORKERS KNOW that it is easy to become stagnant and fall into a routine without even realizing it. You can choose to stagnate or to grow. You can choose mediocrity or mastery. When you shift your attitude about something or someone, you are choosing to grow. When you implement new networking habits that expand the power of your support system, you are choosing mastery. The questions in this chapter were developed by experienced networkers to alert you to possibilities for growth in networking experiences that may come your way.

1. How can I manage my time to network consistently when I am already so busy?

People often think that they don't have time to network and already have too much to do. Yet networking is meant to save time by allowing you to operate more efficiently. With smart and effective self-management, you should be able to accomplish projects and goals in less time and with less effort.

Pay attention whenever you talk with someone, so that you make good use of every conversation. Also, be aware of the people who are already in your support system and fully utilize the opportunities around you. You don't have to go out and find more people to network with; that will happen naturally. You simply need to be more aware of each person who is already in your network.

Ask, listen, and offer support and you will open the door to opportunities all around you. Networking is not "a thing to do" that should take a lot of time. It is the way you interact and relate to people on a daily basis that develops connections or generates opportunities.

197

2. What size network is manageable? Is there a maximum size for maintaining contacts and quality?

The size of your network depends on you and your ability to organize the network well and manage yourself effectively. I have a very large network of people I have met through my speaking engagements who have expressed an interest in being on my mailing list. A smaller portion of my network consists of the core group of friends, associates, and clients with whom I am in touch on a daily or very regular basis. Each level of your network requires different amounts of attention, time, and energy to maintain and grow the relationship. Rather than limiting your support system to a certain size, prioritize your network so that you can utilize and nurture the connections you have at each level in a way that honors that level of relationship.

3. How do I keep track of all the information that is becoming part of my network?

Your list of contacts can be your greatest asset unless it's not well organized; then it can become your greatest nightmare. Many organizational tools are available to help you stay organized and on track with your networking. I use a software program called Priority One to retrieve people by their last name, their company's name, their industry, the club or association they belong to, who introduced them to me, or any combination of eighteen identifiers. This gives me the confidence that comes from having a great deal of information at my fingertips. When I'm going to Denver to conduct a training program, I can send an announcement of my speaking engagements to everyone on my list in the Denver area. If someone asks me for contacts in the environmental industry in Knoxville, Tennessee, I can initiate a computer search to retrieve any contacts that fit that criterion.

It's a good idea to review your organizational tools often to see how to best upgrade and update your list of contacts. Any of the following tools can be utilized to make your networking easier: business card file, Rolodex, spiral notebook, computer software, date planner, or index card file.

You may meet a lot of people and gather a lot of information, but if you don't have a way to retain and recall all of that information, it won't do you or your network any good. Having a system for tracking, organizing, and recalling information is essential to fully utilize your network.

4. What do I do about not remembering people's names?

Stop saying that you can't remember! Our minds have tremendous capabilities, and yet I commonly hear people complaining about having a terrible memory. Memory recall is a skill that anyone can develop. Begin to pay more attention to people. Realize that you can improve your memory if you're willing to practice. Begin to think about the capability of your mind and the value of remembering people. Whenever you start thinking that you can't remember, interrupt that thought and commit to remembering, even if you must stop and write yourself a note about what you want to remember. Develop an attitude of possibility and reinforce it by practicing every day and acknowledging your progress.

David Lallier, who leads the "Don't Forget Memory" Workshop, says that it's not that we can't remember, but that we never got the information in the first place. So often we're thinking about something else when people are talking to us. We seem to be listening and we do hear a few words now and then, but we're not listening in a way that allows us to connect or integrate the information. Giving your full attention to people is the best way to remember who they are, what they do, and what they said.

Attention, association, and repetition are the keys to developing your memory ability. These skills will greatly enhance your self-confidence, your ability to connect with people, and your ability to be a powerful networker. Remembering people and recalling information are vital in introducing people to one another and passing on information to others.

5. How do I develop my ability to connect with people immediately?

An energy or chemistry between people often exists that is unseeable and unexplainable, yet obvious and powerful. It accounts for the times when you meet someone and hit it off immediately. This energy is a driving force behind every encounter, whether it is an interview for a job or a conversation with strangers. Norman York, president of Reedie-York & Associates in Austin, Texas, says, "Anyone in the market today [for a job] is essentially in the chemistry business—the human chemistry business. No matter how much you have to offer in the way of skills and abilities, if you can't relate to the people you meet, the potential value will be lost." You can learn to connect and bond with people by being more aware of the impression you make on others and learning how to naturally find the commonalities, the shared interests, that help you relate to one another.

199

Ask yourself these questions:

• Do you know how to notice when the chemistry is present and when it's missing?

• Do you know how to assess chemistry and work at it over time?

• Can you assess when there simply is not a fit and it is appropriate to call it quits?

• Do you know how to develop an energy that attracts people in a positive manner?

• Do you know what contributes to the energy and chemistry of a relationship?

You probably know intuitively when you hit it off with someone. At the same time it is often easy to tell when there is no connection and you and someone else are not in sync. However, you can take some steps to create an energy that draws people to you, makes you available and approachable, and causes people to feel comfortable with you. What contributes to this energy? Is it your clothes, your confident stature, your tone of voice? It is all of these and more. How you dress, your overall appearance, how you speak, how you treat others, your facial expressions, body language, energy level, attention span, ability to listen, behaviors—all contribute to the way people perceive you and respond to you.

Be aware of your energy level. Your posture, tone of voice, and handshake all convey confidence or doubt, strength or lethargy, enthusiasm or skepticism. The way that you listen is also one way that you convey energy. Do you show interest in what others are saying? Is your interest expressed in your attention, your eye contact, and the way you respond to what they are saying? If you are too long-winded, you may come across as self-centered and unfocused.

6. How do I find a good networking club to join? And how can I tell if it's a strong, powerful group?

The ideal way to find a good organization is through networking. Ask your friends, clients, and associates about the organizations they belong to and inquire about organizations that would best suit your needs. Ask the people you admire and respect about their involvement in professional organizations and associations. Ask if you can attend as a visitor. Visit various groups to find the one that has an opening and is the best fit for you. Clubs have different styles, personalities, purposes, and formats. Find one where you enjoy the people and would look forward to attending the meetings.

A strong group will have regularly scheduled meetings, clear member guidelines, and a board of officers. Its focus should be to provide opportunities to team up with other business professionals and develop relationships that help you build your business and accomplish your professional goals. The structure and purpose of the group is critical. Notice whether a group's purpose is clear and communicated to members regularly and whether the members all seem to be in alignment with it. Are members excited about being there? Is there an energy and camaraderie present at the meetings? Do people speak in a positive and enthusiastic manner? Are they friendly and open while at the same time remaining professional and on purpose? Do they show an interest in you as a guest and prospective member? Do they have a long-term vision? Do they have some people who have been members for a long time? Is there an atmosphere of respect and appreciation? Is it obvious that people are doing business and referring business to one another?

Also find out what's required in terms of time, commitment, and money. Make sure you can give what it takes to make your participation valuable and worthwhile.

Once you join an organization, schedule a meeting with the president or one of the board members to discuss committees, projects, and ideas regarding how you can best get involved to benefit yourself and serve the organization. Remember, it takes a long-term commitment, so don't look for instant referrals. Focus on building relationships—results will happen! Joining and participating over the long term in a powerful networking organization can be one of the wisest and best investments you can make in yourself, your business, and your career.

7. What is a networking focus group and how do I start one?

A networking focus group consists of business owners who all sell to the same market and who meet at least monthly to share contacts and improve the level and quality of their businesses. For example, Becky Easley, owner of Jewelry by Becky of Houston, developed a focus group of people who all sell products and services to engaged couples for their engagement and wedding. Think about all of the products and services that are required for people who are making wedding plans: wedding rings; gifts for the bridal party; flowers for the rehearsal party, the engagement party, luncheons, and the wedding; corsages; food for the rehearsal dinner, bridal parties, and the wedding reception; travel plans for out-of-town guests and the honeymoon; music for the wedding and reception; engagement and wedding photos; a department store gift registry; a facial, makeup, and hair styling for the bride and bridal party; tuxedos and dresses for the bridal party and the parents of the bride and groom; invitations and napkins; and organization of the wedding details. Imagine if every time anyone in this focus group had a new client he or she recommended the services of everyone else in the group!

Once you have identified your target market, make a list of other businesses that have the same market. The possibilities are endless; it just requires some creative energy to consider what products and services are used by your target market. The next step is to decide on one person in each category to join the group. Select someone who is well known to you, someone you enjoy and trust, who provides a quality service or product and is open to learning about new ways to support others and his or her own business. Call this person and set up a meeting to discuss your idea. If you get a positive response, you now have a focus group of two! Grow your group gradually to bring in quality people who will help build that networking momentum.

Focus groups normally meet monthly for approximately two hours. The meeting place can rotate to give you a chance to visit the office or place of business of each participant. A good meeting format would be twenty minutes of networking and fellowship followed by a forty-minute presentation by the member who is hosting the evening. The remaining time is reserved for focus group business, discussion of how to sell better to the target market, sharing of referrals, and feedback on the results of previous referrals. This portion of the meeting is meant to be a free-flowing discussion of ideas that will support the businesses of the members.

8. How does mentoring relate to networking?

Mentoring is a type of networking relationship in which one person with special expertise and experience assists in another person's professional advancement. It is very valuable to have one or more mentors in your profession. By developing trusting relationships with these people, you can move forward in your company or profession with greater ease because you have a teacher or master in whose footsteps you can follow. In the past, people apprenticed to learn their trade and in some professions today it is common for people new to an industry to intern with a company as part of their development. Although mentoring is often viewed as a one-way relationship, it is actually a partnership that gives value and satisfaction to the mentor as well as the one who is mentored. Even though the mentor may appear to have greater experience, insight, or expertise, the relationship is built on mutual respect, and both partners contribute and gain valuable insight and support for their personal and professional growth.

9. How do men and women network differently?

Most of the differences in the way men and women network are the result of their distinct personality and communication styles and the gender conditioning that has influenced our society for years. Women can be very powerful networkers because they have a natural tendency to nurture, relate, be supportive, and connect. Women often network automatically and naturally regarding personal issues and situations in their lives. They are now utilizing some of those same relationship-

203

building and communication skills in their careers and are becoming very powerful networkers in their professional endeavors.

Oftentimes, though, women need to learn to *speak up* in a more positive, assertive, and professional manner regarding the value and benefit of who they are and what they do. Women also tend to be easily aware of others' needs and will often find themselves doing for others when they need to be paying attention to their own needs; they have to learn how to balance their tremendous capacity to give with an equal capacity to ask for what they need and to accept the support of others. Some women also tend to speak in a "feeling" terminology, which may prevent them from being taken seriously with their requests and their ideas. They often respond to others as a helper rather than as a resource and must remember that networking is not about doing for others; it is about being a resource.

Men tend to be more direct and comfortable about asking for information and leads in the professional arena because they feel that they deserve support and success. The "good ol' boy" attitude of "you scratch my back and I'll scratch yours" has for years provided the basis for men to feel that it is important, acceptable, and prestigious to develop a powerful camaraderie with other businessmen. They need to move beyond the "good ol' boy" style of networking, however, to build a more inclusive, diverse support system. Rather than operating from a "keeping score" mentality, they will gain from developing their relationship-building and listening skills. Many men have the ability to be very focused on their goals and objectives, which means that they can be clear and effective in asking for and getting what they want. They simply need to make sure that they are also balancing that strength with the ability to honor and build relationships that lead to satisfaction and fulfillment in all areas of life. Men are learning to appreciate not just the results that can be gained from networking but the intangible, life-enhancing value of a strong personal and professional support system.

It is more important to be aware of others' communication styles and personalities than to concentrate on gender differences. Type A personalities will not want to listen to a lot of verbiage: they want the bottom line—to know what you need and how they can help. With people who are more oriented to relating and connecting, you will need to spend more time developing rapport before you can get to the details of what's needed and wanted.

Don't prejudge people on the basis of gender to predict whether they can or cannot be a valuable part of your network. Instead, approach people as equals in terms of networking and give both women and men the opportunity to be networking resources in your life.

10. How do I make sure my networking is not perceived as flirting?

In order to be professional and avoid misunderstandings about your intentions, you must be very aware of everything you communicate through your tone of voice, eye contact, and body language. Compliments on people's appearance, a suggestive tone of voice, sensual body language, lingering eye contact, and getting personal too quickly can all be perceived as flirting. Be professional with your tone of voice, your body language, and the topics you discuss so that you can develop quality professional networking relationships with both genders.

11. What's the difference between network marketing and networking?

Network marketing is the name used to refer to companies that are set up in a multilevel marketing format. These companies have a multilevel compensation plan that supports their direct sales marketing approach. Distributors or representatives bring in others, who in turn bring in others, and on and on. This concept was first started back in 1945 when Dr. Carl Rehnborg took NutriLite, which was once California Vitamins, and established it as a multilevel operation. Two of his superstars, Jay Van Andel and Rich DeVos, eventually left to start their own business, called Amway, which has grown to a multi-billion-dollar business with over two million distributors in over sixty countries. Other successful companies based on the direct sales or multilevel approach include Mary Kay Cosmetics, Shaklee, Reliv, Melaleuca, Matol Botanical, Oxyfress, Quorum, Avon, and Jewelway. Network marketing companies today sell everything from vitamins to long-distance service to pagers to satellite training programs.

The art and skill of networking is valuable as a marketing tool for any industry. Networking obviously plays a key role in the network marketing firms because the basis of their success is bringing other people into the business and training them to grow and build their business. To succeed in the network marketing industry requires strong relationship building, networking skills, enthusiasm, dedication, and commitment.

12. Is technology going to replace our familiar ways of networking?

Technology is providing many new means of accessing data, communicating with people, and conveying information worldwide. All of this can make it even easier to be in communication with lots of people and share information quickly and efficiently. I now use the computer not only to help me keep track of my network, but also as a vehicle for contacting people, staying in touch, accessing large volumes of information, and creating greater reach and visibility for myself and my business.

With some training, you can learn to access bulletin boards, newsgroups, and on-line forums to network, prospect, gather information, and develop rapport in cyberspace. Technology is not replacing our normal means of networking; instead it is providing new tools for communicating and building relationships. The truth is that the more high-tech we get, the more touch we'll require. Nothing will ever replace the human need for a sense of personal connection. The best approach is to learn the appropriate etiquette for voice mail, the Internet, and other new means of communication; to use the technology wisely; and to let these tools enhance your networking ease and opportunities.

NETWORKING SUCCESS: NOW IT'S UP TO YOU

*66 **T**he last of the human freedoms—to choose one's own attitude in any given set of circumstances, to choose one's own way. 99*

—Viktor Frankl

EVEN THOUGH SUCCESS CAN BE defined in many different ways, I believe we are all yearning for an experience of valued accomplishment, loving relationships, self-value, and a sense of belonging. Many people in our culture have obtained tremendous outward success and yet still struggle with an inner hunger for truly healthy, nurturing, supportive relationships.

Elaine Gray, president of The Success Coach, focuses on helping people achieve "authentic success." By adding the word *authentic,* we are defining a success that is real, not imaginary, genuine, not an imitation, fulfilling, not partially satisfying, and heartwarming! Apparent success can be shallow, yet authentic success is deep, profound, and all-encompassing. Authentic success springs from the relationships we have with others in our lives.

"There is no authentic success separate from mutually empowering relationships," Gray says. "Equally important as business skills and knowledge, true success and enduring happiness result from being affirmed, and given truthful and compassionate feedback." Authentic success is available to all of us if we choose it. "Our ability to become authentically successful occurs spontaneously and naturally when we open ourselves to support from those who are committed to our success," Gray explains. "True quantum improvements, both internally and externally, occur when we allow ourselves to be real, vulnerable and supportable."

This is your life. It is up to you to do what you want with it. It is up to you to choose authentic success, success that enriches all aspects of who you are and encompasses all the relationships that give depth to your life. Philosophers, psychologists, and spiritual teachers throughout time have searched for the prescription for a happy life. David McNally recommends that you ask yourself two simple questions each night before you go to sleep: "Did I today, in some way, grow as a human being?" and "Did I today, in any way, make the world a better place in which to live?" If, more often than not, you can answer yes to these questions, then you will experience a rich, rewarding life of success and happiness.

The opposite of success and happiness is an emptiness, where there is no meaning, no sense of purpose, no experience of growth and accomplishment. Our potential for success and happiness comes from our ability to reach within our heart and soul to find peace and purpose in life. McNally says, "Clearly, what distinguishes truly successful people is that they are contributors. They are in love with life and all the possibilities of what it means to be human. Their accomplishments, their successes, are rooted in their desire to grow and be of service."

You must discover and define success for yourself. You are the only one who knows what is ultimately most satisfying to your heart and soul and helpful to your growth. A ship sailing on the sea continually adjusts and readjusts its direction in ways that the untrained eye will not even notice. And yet those adjustments ensure that the ship will stay on course to reach its destination. You must constantly be aware, alert, and

209

willing to adjust your thoughts, behaviors, and actions and thus guide yourself along the path of authentic success. Others may not notice many of the adjustments and growing pains that you go through to keep yourself on track to success. However, you can be deeply aware of and appreciative of yourself and the courage it takes to adjust day-to-day to the call of authentic success.

Success today is not just a matter of what we accomplish but the overall process and positive experience of our relationships, our accomplishments, our values, and our sense of self. Authentic success includes pride and appreciation, accomplishment and relationships. It encompasses all aspects of our lives.

Authentic success is not a destination. It is a journey of discovery. It is an adventure like no other. It provides the opportunity for human beings to discover how to journey through this life with honor and self-respect. It comes from your heart and your head. It touches everything about you, your network, and your world.

NOTES

See Bibliography for complete details on works cited.

Page

21   *According to epidemiologist Lisa Berkman:* The Berkman, House, Institute for the Advancement of Health, and Luks studies are reported in Kathy Keeton, p. 188.

24   Jeffrey Gitomer, p. 143.

31   Susan Jeffers, *Dare to Connect,* p. 38.

40   *The power of interdependence:* Stephen Covey, p. 49. *Covey describes interdependence:* p. 51.

53   Richard Weylman, p. 238.

62–63   Shad Helmstetter, p. 20.

63   Kenneth Blanchard, p. 44.

65   Tom Peters, *The Pursuit of Wow!* pp. 28–29.

65   Fred Bauer, pp. 72–75.

85   David McNally, p. 21.

94   Anne Baber and Lynne Waymon, p. 4.

95   Larry King, pp. 40–41.

96–97   Max Gunther, p. 125. *Gunther gives a telling example of two women:* pp. 128–132.

100   *Larry King emphasizes:* p. 220. *"Whether you're sitting":* p. 218.

125   Leslie Smith, p. 48.

141   Robyn Davidson in Anne Wilson Schaef, September 10, n.p.

143–144   Stephen Covey, p. 143. *"Make a promise and keep it"*: p. 92. *"By making and keeping promises"*: p. 92. *As Covey says:* p. 217.

155   George Leonard, p. 5.

171   Scott Peck, p. 23.

185   Ivan Misner, p. 72.

185   Richard Weylman, pp. 88–89.

199   Norman York, n.p.

205   The source of the story on NutriLite and Amway's founders was *Upline Magazine,* December 1994, p. 17. Amway business statistics are from Hoover's MasterList Database 1995 and Hoover's Handbook Database (Austin, Tex.: Reference Press).

209   David McNally, p. 49. *McNally says:* p. 43.

BIBLIOGRAPHY

Books

Allenbaugh, Eric. *Wake-Up Calls: You Don't Have to Sleepwalk Through Your Life, Love, or Career!* Austin, Tex.: Discovery Publications, 1992.

Allman, William F. *The Stone Age Present.* New York: Simon & Schuster, 1994.

Arapakis, Maria. *SoftPower.* New York: Warner Books, 1990.

Baber, Anne, and Lynne Waymon. *Great Connections: Small Talk and Networking for Businesspeople.* Manassas Park, Va.: Impact Publications, 1992.

Baker, Wayne E. *Networking Smart: How to Build Relationships for Personal and Organizational Success.* New York: McGraw-Hill, 1994.

Blanchard, Kenneth. *The One Minute Manager.* New York: Morrow, 1982.

Chopra, Deepak. *The Seven Spiritual Laws of Success.* San Rafael, Calif.: Amber-Allen Publishing and New World Publishing, 1993.

Covey, Stephen R. *The 7 Habits of Highly Effective People.* New York: Fireside Books, 1989.

Csikszentmihalyi, Mihaly. *Flow: The Psychology of Optimal Experience.* New York: Harper Perennial, 1990.

Edwards, Paul, Sarah Edwards, and Laura Clampitt Douglas. *Getting Business to Come to You.* New York: Jeremy P. Tarcher/Putnam, 1990.

Fisher, Donna, and Sandy Vilas. *Power Networking: 55 Secrets for Personal and Professional Success.* Austin, Tex.: MountainHarbour Publications, 1993.

Gunther, Max. *The Luck Factor: Why Some People Are Luckier Than Others and How You Can Become One of Them.* New York: Ballantine Books, 1977.

Helmstetter, Shad. *What to Say When You Talk to Yourself.* New York: Pocket Books, 1982.

Jeffers, Susan. *Dare to Connect: Reaching Out in Romance, Friendship and the Workplace.* New York: Ballantine Books, 1993.

Jeffers, Susan. *Feel the Fear and Do It Anyway.* New York: Ballantine Books, 1987.

Keeton, Kathy. *Longevity: The Science of Staying Young.* New York: Viking Penguin, 1992.

King, Larry, with Bill Gilbert. *How to Talk to Anyone, Anytime, Anywhere.* New York: Crown Publishers, 1994.

Leonard, George. *Mastery: The Keys to Success and Long-Term Fulfillment.* New York: Plume, 1992.

Levinson, Jay Conrad. *Guerrilla Marketing Excellence: The Fifty Golden Rules for Small-Business Success.* Boston: Houghton Mifflin, 1993.

Lowstuter, Clyde C., and David P. Robertson. *Network Your Way to Your Next Job . . . Fast.* New York: McGraw-Hill, 1995.

McNally, David. *Even Eagles Need a Push: Learning to Soar in a Changing World.* New York: Dell, 1990.

Misner, Ivan R. *The World's Best-Known Marketing Secret: Building Your Business with Word-of-Mouth Marketing.* Austin, Tex.: Bard & Stephen, 1994.

Nichols, Michael P. *The Lost Art of Listening.* New York: The Guilford Press, 1995.

Oakley, Ed, and Doug Krug. *Enlightened Leadership.* Denver: Stone Tree Publishing, 1991.

Peck, Scott. *Further Along the Road Less Traveled.* New York: Simon & Schuster, 1993.

Peters, Tom. *The Pursuit of Wow! Every Person's Guide to Topsy-Turvy Times.* New York: Vintage Books, 1994.

Putman, Anthony. *Marketing Your Services: A Step-by-Step Guide for Small Businesses and Professionals.* New York: Wiley, 1990.

Quigley, Joseph V. *Vision: How Leaders Develop It, Share It, & Sustain It.* New York: McGraw-Hill, 1993.

Robbins, Anthony. *Unlimited Power: The New Science of Personal Achievement.* New York: Simon & Schuster, 1986.

Rohn, Jim. *The Treasury of Quotes by Jim Rohn, America's Foremost Business Philosopher.* Irving, Tex.: Jim Rohn International, 1994.

Schaef, Anne Wilson. *Meditations for Women Who Do Too Much.* New York: Harper Hazelden, 1990.

Stanley, Thomas J. *Networking with the Affluent and Their Advisors.* Homewood, Ill.: Irwin Business One, 1993.

Tannen, Deborah. *You Just Don't Understand: Men and Women in Conversation.* New York: Morrow, 1990.

Vitale, Joe. *AMA Complete Guide to Small Business Advertising.* New York: American Marketing Association, 1994.

Weylman, C. Richard. *Opening Closed Doors: Keys to Reaching Hard-to-Reach People.* New York: Irwin Professional Publishing, 1994.

Articles

Abrams, Rhonda. "Doing Lunch More Than Just Having a Meal," *The Houston Post,* n.d., 1994.

Bauer, Fred. "The Power of a Note," *Reader's Digest,* December 1991.

Gitomer, Jeffrey. "Good Connections," *Entrepreneur,* November 1994.

Peters, Tom. "Power," *Success,* November 1994.

Smith, Leslie. "How to Avoid Telephone Networking Blunders," *Executive Female,* March/April 1991.

York, Norman. "Networking Requires Hard Work," *Austin Business Journal* 13, no. 12, May 1993.

INDEX

ABOUT THE AUTHOR

DONNA FISHER, president of Discovery Seminars, is a corporate trainer, business consultant, and motivational speaker on the people skills that are vital for success in this high-tech world. She believes individuals control their own success every day through their attitude, communication skills, and professionalism. Her focus is to inspire people to enhance their personal power and effectiveness.

With her background in sales, marketing, and management with Exxon, McDonnell Douglas, the Houston Center for Attitudinal Healing and the University of Houston, she understands her clients' challenges and needs. Her keynote presentations and workshops are featured at events ranging from regional sales meetings to international conferences and conventions. Her energizing, information-packed programs have been scheduled for return engagements with such companies as Chase Bank, Arthur Andersen, Ernst & Young, and Lucent Technologies.

When you schedule Donna for a program, you have chosen one of only 295 speakers worldwide who have earned the Certified Speaking Professional (CSP) designation from the National Speakers Association. Her first book, *Power Networking: 55 Secrets for Personal and Professional Success,* coauthored with Sandy Vilas, has been translated into four languages and recommended by *Time* magazine. Donna has created and performed on audio- and videotapes derived from her books. Her information is also available through articles that have been published in the *Wall Street Journal,* the *Chicago Tribune, Business Start-Ups,* and other major publications.

**Visit your favorite bookstore
for additional copies of *People Power*.**

**For special orders and bulk purchases,
call toll-free
(800) 934-9675.**

ORDER FORM

Quantity		Price	Total

*People Power: 12 Power Principles
to Enrich Your Business, Career &
Personal Networks*

| | Paperback | $14.95 | $ _____ |

*Power Networking: 55 Secrets for
Personal & Professional Success*

by Donna Fisher and Sandy Vilas

_____	Paperback	14.95	$ _____
_____	Hardcover	24.95	$ _____
_____	Audiotape set (4 tapes) by Donna Fisher	19.95	$ _____

The Ten Commandments of Networking

| _____ | Audiotape by Donna Fisher | 10.95 | _____ |
| _____ | Video by Donna Fisher | 59.95 | _____ |

Tax (Texas residents only) _____

Shipping and handling ($4.00 on first item; 50¢ each addl. item) _____

QUANTITY DISCOUNTS ARE AVAILABLE ON BULK PURCHASES	**TOTAL** $ _____

Name _____

( )

Company _____ Phone # _____

Address _____ City _____ State _____ Zip _____

American Express, MasterCard, or VISA # _____ Exp. Date _____

Signature _____

**To order books or for information about workshops, seminars, presentations,
and corporate trainings call: Donna Fisher, 6524 San Felipe, PMB #138, Houston,
Texas 77057-2611; (713) 267-3914, (800) 934-9675. www.donnafisher.com**